NMTA

History, Geography, Economics, Civics and Government
Skill Practice

Practice Test Questions for the NMTA Test

COMPLETE
TEST PREPARATION INC.
WWW.TEST-PREPARATION.CA

Published by
Complete Test Preparation Inc.

Visit us on the web at https://www.test-preparation.ca
Printed in the USA

ISBN-13: 978-1772450354 (Complete Test Preparation Inc.)
ISBN-10: 1772450359

Version 9 April 2025

About Complete Test Preparation

Why Us?
The Complete Test Preparation Team has been publishing high quality study materials since 2005, with a catalogue of over 145 titles, in English, French and Chinese, as well as ESL curriculum for all levels.

To keep up with the industry changes, we update everything all the time!

And the best part?
With every purchase, you're helping people all over the world improve themselves and their education. So thank you in advance for supporting this mission with us! Together, we are truly making a difference in the lives of those often forgotten by the system.

Charities that we support
https://www.test-preparation.ca/charities-and-non-profits/

You have definitely come to the right place.
If you want to spend your valuable study time where it will help you the most - we've got you covered today and tomorrow.

Feedback

We welcome your feedback. Email us at feedback@test-preparation.ca with your comments and suggestions. We carefully review all suggestions and often incorporate reader suggestions into upcoming versions. As a Print on Demand Publisher, we update our products frequently.

Contents

The Environment and Sustainability

Environmental consciousness is important for the continued growth of our company. In addition to eco-balancing each title, as a print on demand publisher, we only print units as orders come in, which greatly reduces excess printing and waste. This revolutionary printing technology also eliminates carbon emissions from trucks hauling boxes of books everywhere to warehouses. We also maintain a commitment to recycling any waste materials that may result from the printing process. We continue to review our manufacturing practices on an ongoing basis to ensure we are doing our part to protect and improve the environment.

Getting Started

ONGRATULATIONS! **By deciding to take the** NMTA History, Geography, Economics, Civics and Government, you have taken the first step toward a great future! Of course, there is no point in taking this important examination unless you intend to do your very best in order to earn the highest grade you possibly can. That means getting yourself organized and discovering the best approaches, methods and strategies to master the material. Yes, that will require real effort and dedication on your part but if you are willing to focus your energy and devote the study time necessary, before you know it you will be on you will be passing your exam with a great mark!

We know that taking on a new endeavour can be scary, and it is easy to feel unsure of where to begin. That's where we come in. This study guide is designed to help you improve your test-taking skills, show you a few tricks of the trade

and increase both your competency and confidence.

About the Exam

The NMTA Test is composed of four main sections, US and world history, geography, social science methods and concepts and economics. The exam is computer based. See below for tips on taking a computer based exam.

While we seek to make our guide as comprehensive as possible, note that like all exams, the NMTA Test might be adjusted at some future point. New material might be added, or content that is no longer relevant or applicable might be removed. It is always a good idea to give the materials you receive when you register to take the NMTA a careful review.

The NMTA History, Geography, Economics, Civics and Government Study Plan

Now that you have made the decision to take the NMTA, it is time to get started. Before you do another thing, you will need to figure out a plan of attack. The very best study tip is to start early! The longer the time period you devote to regular study practice, the more likely you will be to retain the material and be able to access it quickly. If you thought that 1x20 is the same as 2x10, guess what? It really is not, when it comes to study time. Reviewing material for just an hour per day over the course of 20 days is far better than studying for two hours a day for only 10 days. The more often you revisit a particular piece of information, the better you will know it. Not only will your grasp and understanding be better, but your ability to reach into your brain and quickly and efficiently pull out the tidbit you need, will be greatly enhanced as well.

The great Chinese scholar and philosopher Confucius believed that true knowledge could be defined as knowing both what you know and what you do not know. The first step in preparing for the NMTA is to assess your strengths and weaknesses.

Making a Study Schedule

To make your study time most productive you will need to develop a study plan. The purpose of the plan is to organize all the bits of pieces of information in such a way that you will not feel overwhelmed. Rome was not built in a day, and learning everything you will need to know to pass the NMTA is going to take time, too. Arranging the material you need to learn into manageable chunks is the best way to go. Each study session should make you feel as though you have succeeded in accomplishing your goal, and your goal is simply to learn what you planned to learn during that particular session. Try to organize the content in such a way that each study session builds on previous ones. That way, you will retain the information, be better able to access it, and review the previous bits and pieces at the same time.

Self-assessment

The Best Study Tip! The very best study tip is to start early! The longer you study regularly, the more you will retain and 'learn' the material. Studying for 1 hour per day for 20 days is far better than studying for 2 hours for 10 days.

What don't you know?

The first step is to assess your strengths and weaknesses. You may already have an idea of where your weaknesses are, or you can take our Self-assessment modules for each of the areas, Reading Comprehension, Arithmetic, Essay Writing, Algebra and College Level Math.

Exam Component	Rate 1 to 5
History	
US History	
World History	
Geography	
Social Science Methods and Concepts	
Economics	

Making a Study Schedule

The key to a study plan is to divide the material you need to learn into manageable size and learn it, while at the same time reviewing the material that you already know.

Using the table above, any scores of three or below, you need to spend time learning, going over and practicing this subject area. A score of four means you need to review the material, but you don't have to spend time re-learning. A score of five and you are OK with just an occasional review before the exam.

A score of zero or one means you really do need to work on this and you should allocate the most time and give it the highest priority. Some students prefer a 5-day plan and others a 10-day plan. It also depends on how much time you have until the exam.

Here is an example of a 5-day plan based on an example from the table above:

US History: 1   Study 1 hour everyday – review on last day
World History: 3   Study 1 hour for 2 days then ½ hour and then review
Geography: 4   Review every second day
Economics: 2 Study 1 hour on the first day – then ½ hour everyday
Social Science Methods and Concepts: 5   Review for ½ hour every other day

Using this example, economics and Social Science Methods and Concepts are good and only need occasional review. Geography is good and needs 'some' review. World History need a bit of work and US History is very weak and need most of the time. Based on this, here is a sample study plan:

Day	Subject	Time
Monday		
Study	US History	1 hour
Study	Economics	1 hour
	½ hour break	
Study	World History	1 hour
Review	Geography	½ hour
Tuesday		
Study	US History	1 hour
Study	Economics	½ hour
	½ hour break	
Study	World History	½ hour
Review	Geography	½ hour
Wednesday		
Study	US History	1 hour
Study	Economics	½ hour
	½ hour break	
Study	World History	½ hour
Thursday		
Study	US History	½ hour
Study	Economics	½ hour
Review	World History	½ hour
	½ hour break	
Review	Geography	½ hour
Friday		
Review	US History	½ hour
Review	Economics	½ hour
Review	World History	½ hour
	½ hour break	
Review	Geography	½ hour
Review	Economics	½ hour

Using this example, adapt the study plan to your own schedule. This schedule assumes 2 ½ - 3 hours available to study everyday for a 5 day period.

First, write out what you need to study and how much. Next figure out how many days you have before the test. Note, do NOT study on the last day before the test. On the last day before the test, you won't learn anything and will probably only confuse yourself.

Make a table with the days before the test and the number of hours you have available to study each day. We suggest working with 1 hour and ½ hour time slots.

Start filling in the blanks, with the subjects you need to study the most getting the most time and the most regular time slots (i.e. everyday) and the subjects that you know getting the least time (e.g. ½ hour every other day, or every 3rd day).

Tips for making a schedule

Once you make a schedule, stick with it! Make your study sessions reasonable. If you make a study schedule and don't stick with it, you set yourself up for failure. Instead, schedule study sessions that are a bit shorter and set yourself up for success! Make sure your study sessions are do-able. Studying is hard work, but after you pass, you can party and take a break!

Schedule breaks. Breaks are just as important as study time. Work out a rotation of studying and breaks that works for you.

Build up study time. If you find it hard to sit still and study for 1 hour straight through, build up to it. Start with 20 minutes, and then take a break. Once you get used to 20-minute study sessions, increase the time to 30 minutes. Gradually work you way up to 1 hour.

40 minutes to 1 hour is optimal. Studying for longer than this is tiring and not productive. Studying for shorter isn't long enough to be productive.

Study Tips for Computer-based tests

The Middle Grades Social Science Test is a Computer based, exam, which is just like the pencil-and-paper exam but digital.

The first tip, which applies to either type of exam, is to use your scratch paper. Computer-based tests do not allow you to jump around. The test questions are displayed in a set sequence. Use your scratch paper to make notes, copy diagrams, or anything else you feel will help you answer the questions that follow.

Other Tips and Strategies

There are several tips and strategies that can help you perform well on both the computer-based and computer-adaptive exams.

Practice. Practicing the test gives you the chance to see the types of questions that are asked, as well as providing you an opportunity to see how the test looks.

Complete the test tutorials. Most exams have a computer tutorial for test-takers immediately before the exam. Make sure you take the time to go through it. The tutorial is not timed, and it will walk you through the process of taking the computer-based exam. Even though you probably know how to use a computer and it may seem unnecessary, do the tutorial. Make sure you know everything you possibly can about what you are about to do!

Be aware of the time. The test is timed. Typically, there is an on-screen clock that counts down the remaining time and alerts you when you are down to five minutes. Pace yourself so you can finish each section in the allotted time.

Practice Test Questions Set 1

The questions below are not the same as you will find on the NMTA History, Geography, Economics, Civics and Government - that would be too easy! And nobody knows what the questions will be and they change all the time. **Below are general questions that cover the same subject areas as the NMTA test and are intended for skill practice only.** So, while the format and exact wording of the questions may differ slightly, and change from year to year, if you can answer the questions below, you will have no problem with the NMTA test.

For the best results, take these practice test questions as if it were the real exam. Set aside time when you will not be disturbed, and a location that is quiet and free of distractions. Read the instructions carefully, read each question carefully, and answer to the best of your ability.
Use the bubble answer sheets provided. When you have completed the practice questions, check your answer against the Answer Key and read the explanation provided.

Do not attempt more than one set of practice test questions in one day. After completing the first practice test, wait two or three days before attempting the second set of questions.

World History Answer Sheet

	A	B	C	D	E			A	B	C	D	E
1	○	○	○	○	○		21	○	○	○	○	○
2	○	○	○	○	○		22	○	○	○	○	○
3	○	○	○	○	○		23	○	○	○	○	○
4	○	○	○	○	○		24	○	○	○	○	○
5	○	○	○	○	○		25	○	○	○	○	○
6	○	○	○	○	○		26	○	○	○	○	○
7	○	○	○	○	○		27	○	○	○	○	○
8	○	○	○	○	○		28	○	○	○	○	○
9	○	○	○	○	○		29	○	○	○	○	○
10	○	○	○	○	○		30	○	○	○	○	○
11	○	○	○	○	○							
12	○	○	○	○	○							
13	○	○	○	○	○							
14	○	○	○	○	○							
15	○	○	○	○	○							
16	○	○	○	○	○							
17	○	○	○	○	○							
18	○	○	○	○	○							
19	○	○	○	○	○							

US History Answer Sheet

	A	B	C	D	E			A	B	C	D	E
1	○	○	○	○	○		21	○	○	○	○	○
2	○	○	○	○	○		22	○	○	○	○	○
3	○	○	○	○	○		23	○	○	○	○	○
4	○	○	○	○	○		24	○	○	○	○	○
5	○	○	○	○	○		25	○	○	○	○	○
6	○	○	○	○	○		26	○	○	○	○	○
7	○	○	○	○	○		27	○	○	○	○	○
8	○	○	○	○	○		28	○	○	○	○	○
9	○	○	○	○	○		29	○	○	○	○	○
10	○	○	○	○	○		30	○	○	○	○	○
11	○	○	○	○	○
12	○	○	○	○	○
13	○	○	○	○	○
14	○	○	○	○	○
15	○	○	○	○	○
16	○	○	○	○	○
17	○	○	○	○	○
18	○	○	○	○	○
19	○	○	○	○	○
20	○	○	○	○	○

Geography Answer Sheet

	A	B	C	D	E
1	○	○	○	○	○
2	○	○	○	○	○
3	○	○	○	○	○
4	○	○	○	○	○
5	○	○	○	○	○
6	○	○	○	○	○
7	○	○	○	○	○
8	○	○	○	○	○
9	○	○	○	○	○
10	○	○	○	○	○
11	○	○	○	○	○
12	○	○	○	○	○
13	○	○	○	○	○
14	○	○	○	○	○
15	○	○	○	○	○
16	○	○	○	○	○
17	○	○	○	○	○
18	○	○	○	○	○
19	○	○	○	○	○
20	○	○	○	○	○

Social Science Methodology Answer Sheet

```
        A  B  C  D  E
    1  ○  ○  ○  ○  ○
    2  ○  ○  ○  ○  ○
    3  ○  ○  ○  ○  ○
    4  ○  ○  ○  ○  ○
    5  ○  ○  ○  ○  ○
    6  ○  ○  ○  ○  ○
    7  ○  ○  ○  ○  ○
    8  ○  ○  ○  ○  ○
    9  ○  ○  ○  ○  ○
   10  ○  ○  ○  ○  ○
   11  ○  ○  ○  ○  ○
   12  ○  ○  ○  ○  ○
   13  ○  ○  ○  ○  ○
   14  ○  ○  ○  ○  ○
   15  ○  ○  ○  ○  ○
   16  ○  ○  ○  ○  ○
   17  ○  ○  ○  ○  ○
   18  ○  ○  ○  ○  ○
   19  ○  ○  ○  ○  ○
   20  ○  ○  ○  ○  ○
```

Economics Answer Sheet

	A	B	C	D	E
1	○	○	○	○	○
2	○	○	○	○	○
3	○	○	○	○	○
4	○	○	○	○	○
5	○	○	○	○	○
6	○	○	○	○	○
7	○	○	○	○	○
8	○	○	○	○	○
9	○	○	○	○	○
10	○	○	○	○	○
11	○	○	○	○	○
12	○	○	○	○	○
13	○	○	○	○	○
14	○	○	○	○	○
15	○	○	○	○	○
16	○	○	○	○	○
17	○	○	○	○	○
18	○	○	○	○	○
19	○	○	○	○	○
20	○	○	○	○	○

Part I - World History

1. What is an early human civilization that smelted copper and alloyed it with tin?

    a. The Tin Age

    b. The Bronze Age

    c. The Stone Age

    d. The Iron Age

2. Which of these are NOT a trait of Classical Greece (4th and 5th centuries BCE)?

    a. The Punic Wars

    b. The Persian Wars

    c. The Parthenon

    d. The philosopher Socrates

3. What political practice, that still influences governments today, was started in Classical Greece?

    a. Dictatorship

    b. Communism

    c. Capitalism

    d. Democracy

4. What are Ares, Aphrodite, Demeter and Athena examples of?

    a. Greek gods

    b. Roman gods

    c. Egyptian gods

    d. Norse gods

5. Which of these did NOT contribute to the fall of the Roman Empire?

    a. The spread of Christianity

    b. Political instability

    c. Invasion by Egyptian forces

    d. Over reliance on slave labor

6. What is/are the Vedas in ancient Indian history?

    a. A time period in which the region saw great economic, social and religious freedom.

    b. The ruling class

    c. A group of people who took over the original Harappan people of India.

    d. Texts discussing the history and religion of Indian peoples and transmitted orally.

7. What was the first recorded Chinese dynasty?

    a. Xia Dynasty

    b. Han Dynasty

    c. Tang Dynasty

    d. Qing Dynasty

8. Which of these inventions were NOT invented by the Chinese?

    a. Paper making

    b. Chemical warfare

    c. Gunpowder

    d. Calculus

9. Which religion allows people to follow the Eightfold Path to Nirvana?

    a. Buddhism

    b. Hinduism

    c. Islam

    d. Taoism

10. What major religion emerged through the prophet Muhammad in Arabia in 7th century CE?

    a. Christianity

    b. Islam

    c. Judaism

    d. Zoroastrianism

11. Which of these factors was NOT important in the development of European Nation States?

    a. Breaking of the Catholic Church from the state in England

    b. Establishment of national languages

    c. Napoleon Bonaparte in France

    d. Centralization of European governments

12. Which of the following was the main reason for mass migrations into Western Europe during the Dark Ages?

    a. Violence in Eastern Europe that caused people to flee

    b. Rapid increases in population that forced people to migrate

    c. Economic and agricultural prosperity in Rome that encouraged others to move there

    d. Refusal of Roman elite to support the military that would have stopped migration

13. Which invention was a cause of the Renaissance in Europe?

a. The steam engine which allowed mass transportation of goods

b. The flying shuttle which increased cloth production

c. The printing press which increased production of books

d. Concave and convex lenses which led to the development of eye glasses, microscopes, and telescopes

14. Which important Renaissance figure wrote Utopia?

a. Thomas More

b. Niccolo Machiavelli

c. Martin Luther

d. Nicholas Copernicus

15. Which of these was NOT a result of the Renaissance in Europe?

a. Increased appreciation for reason, the arts and sciences.

b. Weakening of the authority of the Church.

c. Weakening of the authority of the monarchy.

d. Increased the use of local languages.

16. What did an increased spirit of inquiry by the people, interference by the Pope in non-religious matters and selling of indulgences by the Church led to?

a. The Renaissance

b. The Reformation

c. The Scientific Revolution

d. The Protestant Revolution

17. Which of these was NOT a result of the Reformation?

a. The creation of the Protestant sect of the Christian Church

b. The Thirty Years' War

c. Increased power of the monarchy

d. An end to religious prosecution

18. What is Martin Luther most famous for?

a. Breaking free of the Church and supporting the formation of Presbyterian churches

b. Preaching for religious tolerance during the Reformation

c. Writing the 95 theses in 1517 that attacked the Church

d. Writing Utopia in 1516

19. Which key figure of the Scientific Revolution was responsible for the discovery of the laws of planetary motion that later influenced Isaac Newton?

a. Johannes Kepler

b. Galileo Galilei

c. Francis Bacon

d. Rene Descartes

20. Who introduced the heliocentric view of the universe?

a. Nicholas Copernicus

b. Tycho Brahe

c. Francis Bacon

d. Isaac Newton

21. Which of these did NOT lead to the Scientific Revolution in Europe?

    a. Expansion of trade

    b. Humanism

    c. The Reformation

    d. Need for military advancement

22. What was the main reason for European exploration in Asia?

    a. Spreading Christianity

    b. Trading and acquiring goods

    c. Need for slaves

    d. Acquisition of land

23. Which of these was NOT a major result of European colonization of Africa?

    a. Lack of manufacturing

    b. Civil war

    c. Poverty

    d. Pollution

24. What was NOT a reason European countries decided to create colonies in Asia and Africa?

    a. Excess population

    b. Desire for wealth

    c. Fear of attacks by Asia or Africa

    d. National prestige

25. Which were the first European powers to colonize the Americas?

   a. England and France

   b. Spain and France

   c. Spain and Portugal

   d. England and Portugal

26. What was the leading cause of death in indigenous peoples following European colonization in the Americas?

   a. Warfare

   b. Disease

   c. Starvation

   d. Slavery

27. What period of history was the Middle Kingdom (2040-1786 BC)?

   a. Ancient Egyptian

   b. Ancient Roman

   c. Ancient Chinese

   d. Ancient Sumerian

28. Where did civilization first appear in the world?

   a. Egypt

   b. Mesopotamia

   c. Africa

   d. China

29. Who was the first Emperor of Rome?

a. Julius Caesar

b. Claudius

c. Augustus

d.Nero

30. Which dynasty marks the beginning of Imperial China?

a. Qing dynasty

b. Sui dynasty

c. Xia dynasty

d. Qin dynasty

31. What is the ancient Chinese belief that heaven granted emperors the right to rule because their ability to be just and fair.

a. The Mandate of God

b. The Mandate of China

c. The Mandate of Heaven

d. The Chinese Mandate

32. Who fought in the Punic Wars?

a. Rome and Egypt

b. Rome and Carthage

c. Egypt and Carthage

d. None of the above

33. Who was the first Holy Roman Emperor?

a. Louis I

b. Charles II

c. Lothair I

d. Charlemagne

34. Mary I of England, known as Bloody Mary, is the daughter of which king?

a. Henry V

b. Henry VI

c. Henry VIII

d. Charles II

35. The French Revolution began in which year?

a. 1787

b. 1789

c. 1790

d. 1799

Part II - US History

1. Which one of these was not part of the Intolerable Acts?

a. The Stamp Act

b. The Townshed Acts

c. The Tea Act

d. The Foreign Trade Act

2. The British American colonists revolted because

a. most colonists wanted to be free from British rule.

b. most colonists wanted to be represented in Parliament.

c. most colonists did not want to be taxed.

d. All of the Above

3. Why did the British Parliament impose the first of the Intolerable Acts?

a. To raise revenue for British Parliamentary salaries

b. To pay for the British military in the American Colonies

c. To make trade with non-British countries more expensive

d. To fund the British military's ongoing war in India

4. What was the last plea to Great Britain to avert the American Revolutionary War?

a. The Olive Branch Petition

b. The Dove Accords

c. Jefferson's Plea

d. Adam's Plea

5. Why did the First Continental Congress meet?

a. Respond to the Intolerable Acts

b. Establish a military

c. Establish a federal government

d. Address issues of states rights

6. Why did the Second Continental Congress meet?

a. Establish a federal government

b. Respond to the Intolerable Acts

c. Ask for aid from the French

d. Establish a military

7. What document announced a state of war between the British American colonists and Great Britain?

a. The Articles of Confederation

b. The Declaration of Independence

c. The United States Constitution

d. The Declaration of Hostilities

8. Which of these was NOT considered part of Manifest Destiny?

a. American people and institutions are special

b. America had a mission to turn the west into an agrarian landscape

c. America's destiny was to settle the west

d. All of the above are correct

9. What was the start of western expansion?

a. The Clermont steamboat

b. The Mexican American War

c. The invention of the telegraph

d. The discovery of gold in California

10. When did the Gold Rush start in California?

a. 1849

b. 1848

c. 1855

d. 1851

11. Which was the largest land acquisition for the United States?

    a. The Louisiana Purchase

    b. The Treaty of Guadalupe Hidalgo

    c. The Texas Annexation

    d. The Gadsden Purchase

12. Which State was once a nation with its own president before joining the Union during westward expansion?

    a. Delaware

    b. California

    c. Alaska

    d. Texas

13. What most shortened the time it took for people to travel across the United States during westward expansion?

    a. The telegraph

    b. The Clearmont steamboat

    c. The Transcontinental Railroad

    d. The Northwest Passage

14. What marked the end of western expansion?

    a. Arizona statehood

    b. The end of the Mexican American War

    c. The Completion Speech

    d. The President William Mckinley's Assassination

15. What was the Trail of Tears?

    a. The last bloody battle/retreat of the Sioux Nation westward

    b. The forced removal of Irish immigrants from New York

    c. The relocation of many Native American tribes to "Indian Territory"

    d. Part of the Transcontinental Railroad that claimed the most lives in its building

16. Who did Jacksonian Democrats believe should be able to vote?

    a. White males

    b. All males

    c. Everyone

    d. Landed gentry

17. The Second Great Awakening was

    a. a multi-denominational religious movement to prepare people for the "End of Days."

    b. a Reaction against religion, and the rise of logic over faith.

    c. a religious movement against skepticism and rationalisml

    d. a movement aimed toward reducing corruption in politics and putting politicians in power to support the "everyman."

18. In what case did Chief Justice John Marshal most increase the powers of the Supreme Court?

    a. Fletcher v. Peck

    b. Marbury v. Madison

    c. Brown v. Board of Education

    d. Roe v. Wade

19. Which of these was NOT a purpose of the Lewis and Clark Expedition?

    a. Explore and map the Louisiana purchase

    b. Find a practical route to the Pacific Ocean

    c. Establish American presence in the Louisiana Territory

    d. Try to claim some of the adjoining Spanish territory

20. Which of these is true about the First Barbary War?

    a. The United States fought the war because they were the only country forced to pay a tribute to the Barbary States

    b. It was the first time the United States fought a war in a foreign land

    c. Spain suggested that the United States should fight or the Barbary Pirates would demand more tribute for safe passage

    d. The United States decisively beat the Barbary pirates and took back American prisoners without having to pay any tribute or ransom

21. What is entailed in the Monroe Doctrine?

    a. The suffrage of all white males

    b. The removal of Native Americans from the Deep South

    c. The assertion that the Americas would be free from European influence

    d. The assertion that the United States would act as an arbitrator for any problems that occur in the Americas

22. Which of these states was NOT part of the Confederacy?

    a. West Virginia

    b. Tennessee

    c. Texas

    d. Florida

23. Which of these was NOT a reason the South succeeded from the Union?

a. Slavery

b. Northern commercial competition

c. States rights

d. Tariffs

24. Which below best describes the Missouri Compromise?

a. Missouri would enter the Union as a free state and Texas enter the Union as a slave state

b. It prohibited slavery in the former Louisiana Territory north of 36°30' including Missouri

c. Missouri would enter the Union as a slave state and California would enter as a free state

d. All areas in the former Louisiana Territory north of 36°30' except for Missouri would enter the union as free states

25. What did the Kansas-Nebraska Act do?

a. Close Nebraska to slavery and make Kansas a slave state.

b. It prohibited slavery in the former Louisiana Territory north of 36°30' including Kansas and Nebraska

c. All areas in the former Louisiana Territory north of 36°30' except for Kansas and Nebraska would enter the union as free states

d. The decision of whether Kansas or Nebraska would become either a slave or free state would be determined by popular vote

26. In response to what event did the Confederate States of America form?

a The Emancipation Proclamation

b. Jefferson Davis declaring that the South would no longer bend to the will of the North

c. The election of Abraham Lincoln

d. Robert E. Lee declaring that the South would no longer bend to the will of the North

27. Why did the Confederate States of America believe that European nations would side with them over the United States of America?

a. The North had angered much of Europe by setting up tariffs against manufactured goods.

b. Many of the upper class in the South had family in Europe

c. The South produced much of the cotton that Europe depended on for its textile industries

d. The Confederacy thought that the Europeans would identify more with the genteel South compared to the rough North

28. What was the start of the American Civil War?

a. Abraham Lincoln's election

b. The Confederate attack on Fort Sumter

c. The Battle of Gettysburg

d. The Battle of Antietam

29. Who provided the biggest labor base for the Second Industrial Revolution?

a. European immigrants

b. Children

c. Mexican immigrants

d. African Slaves

30. Which of these resources did NOT play a large part in the United States becoming a major industrial nation in the late 19th century?

    a. Oil

    b. Wood

    c. Rubber

    d. Coal

31. Which of these was NOT a new technology that helped the United States become a major industrial nation in the late 19th century?

    a. Highways

    b. Steel

    c. Railroad

    d. Telegraph

32. Which was true about the Second Industrial Revolution?

    a. Only a few of the richest men, and a few lucky others saw a significant rise in wealth

    b. Due to U.S. dominance domestic tariffs were lowered

    c. The Second Industrial Revolution happened in many countries in Europe and Asia

    d. The Second Industrial Revolution began with the invention of the telegraph

33. Which of these men was NOT a "Robber Baron?"

    a. John Rockefeller

    b. J. P. Morgan

    c. Andrew Carnegie

    d. Samuel Gompers

34. What was the first national labor union?

a. The National Labor Union

b. The Federation of Organized Trades and Labor Unions

c. The Knights of Labor

d. The American Federation of Labor

35. Why did the United States enter the War in the Pacific?

a. They were asked by France for support

b. The Japanese bombed Pearl Harbor

c. Germany declared War on Great Britain, whom the United States was allied to

d. They felt morally compelled to fight against Germany

Part III - Geography

1. Which of the following is not a reason humans move to urban areas?

a. Excitement

b. Education

c. Open spaces

d. Job opportunities

2. The era of human existence before writing was developed is known as

a. Ancient history

b. Prehistory

c. Recorded history

d. Unknown history

3. A thin stretch of land that connects two large areas of land is called

    a. a glacier.

    b. a peninsula.

    c. an isthmus.

    d. an ice sheet.

4. What is an ecosystem?

    a. a group of environmentalists that fight pollution

    b. a group of living organisms and their surrounding environment

    c. a law that delineates city zones

    d. a set of protocols that ensure environmental sustainability

5. Which ocean borders the east coast of Africa?

    a. Atlantic

    b. Indian

    c. Arctic

    d. Pacific

6. Cuba, Haiti and Puerto Rico are located in the

    a. Caribbean Sea.

    b. North Sea.

    c. Indian Ocean.

    d. Black Sea.

7. The Ural Mountains separate the continents of

    a. North and South America.

    b. Africa and Asia.

    c. Australia and Asia.

    d. Europe and Asia.

8. Australia is a very large

    a. continent.

    b. ocean.

    c. island.

    d. peninsula.

9. A nation is also known as

    a. a country.

    b. a government.

    c. a society.

    d. a utopia.

10. Which of the following is shown most clearly on a physical map?

    a. the borders of countries

    b. the movements of various populations

    c. the ruins of ancient civilizations

    d. features such as mountains, lakes and rivers

11. Which of the following is shown most clearly on a political map?

    a. The borders of countries

    b. The movements of various populations

    c. The ruins of ancient civilizations

    d. Features such as mountains, lakes and rivers

12. The study of human movements and the development of society is known as

    a. biology.

    b. archeology.

    c. anthropology.

    d. paleontology.

13. The study of artifacts from the past is known as

    a. biology.

    b. archaeology.

    c. anthropology.

    d. paleontology.

14. The connection of different societies through technology such as the telephone, cellular phone and internet is known as

    a. the first agricultural revolution.

    b. the industrial revolution.

    c. the second agricultural revolution.

    d. the communications revolution.

15. Globalization refers to the

    a. education of all people around the world.

    b. connection of all of the economies of the world.

    c. large colonial empires of England and Spain.

    d. the study of ancient civilizations.

16. What is the top of a mountain is called?

    a. Apex

    b. Crown

    c. Summit

    d. Peak

17. What is the formula for calculating population density?

    a. Total population / Total area

    b. Total population * Total area

    c. Total population + Total area

    d. Total population – Total area

18. What is the best method of instantaneous diffusion in today's modern world?

    a. Internet

    b. Telegraph

    c. Telephone

    d. Sending a letter

19. Countries are best identified as _____ regions.

    a. Formal

    b. Territorial

    c. Functional

    d. Perceptual

20. Language helps us identify _____ regions.

    a. Formal

    b. Territorial

    c. Functional

    d. Perceptual

Part IV Social Studies Skills and Concepts

1. What is the established way groups of people look at philosophical views and religious faith called?

    a, Conflict

    b. Belief Systems

    c. Change

    d. Culture

2. Relying on others in mutually beneficial ways is known as _____.

    a. Interdependence

    b. Empathy

    c. Identity

    d. Choice

3. Individuals given fair treatment in personal, societal, and governmental interactions is called _____.

    a. Power

    b. Empathy

    c. Justice

    d. Citizenship

4. The basic political, social, and economic rights that all humans are entitled to are known as:

    a. Laws

    b. Human Rights

    c. Justice

    d. Values

5. The principles that serve as the foundation for the United States' form of government are called _____.

    a. Justice

    b. Citizenship

    c. Civic Values

    d. Decision Making

6. What is the process we use to influence the many facets of our lives?

    a. Decision Making

    b. Rule Breaking

    c. Rationalizing

    d. Diversifying

7. A politically organized society is run by a _____.

    a. Dictatorship

    b. Oligarchy

    c. Monarchy

    jd. Government

8. Your ability to influence the actions of others refers to your _____.

    a. Citizenship

    b. Power

    c. Influence

    d. Empathy

9. Monarchies, oligarchies, dictatorships, democracies, republics, etc. are all _____.

    a. Political Systems

    b. Negative governments

    c. Positive governments

    d. Effective governments

10. Voting fulfills one of the responsibilities of _____ in the United States.

    a. Justice

    b. Rights

    c. Citizenship

    d. Ruling

11. People who are united by a geographic location or by a political organization are a part of the same _____-state.

    a. Dictatorial

    b. Democratic

    c. Republican

    d. Nation

12. The conflict between our unlimited needs and wants and how many human and natural resources there are to fulfill them is called _____.

    a. Scarcity

    b. Depletion

    c. Destruction

    d. Expenditure

13. _____ is defined as the natural and manmade elements that surround us.

    a. Location

    b. Environment

    c. Geography

    d. Social Studies

14. The study of human activity on earth, including the way human settlement impacts Earth's surface, is called _____.

    a. Human Systems

    b., Human Studies

    c. Globalism

    d. Global Systems

15. _____ systems are the processes that shape Earth's surface. It includes the interaction of plant and animal life.

Geography

Human

Physical

Ecology

Part V - Economics

1. As demand increases, supply tends to

a. decrease.

b. increase.

c. remain the same.

d. fluctuate.

2. As supply increases, prices tend to

a. rise.

b. fall.

c. remain the same.

d. fluctuate.

3. As economy of scale increase, products are

a. expensive to produce at first, but eventually become less expensive.

b. cheap to produce at first, but eventually become more expensive.

c. expensive to produce because they are customized to individual customers.

d. sold to the highest bidder.

4. Which of the following is true of a free market economy?

a. The government owns the resources but allows citizens to own private property.

b. The government owns the resources and does not allow citizens to own private property.

c. Resources and private property are owned by citizens.

d. Resources are owned by citizens, but not private property.

5. Which of the following is true of a command economy?

a. The government owns the resources but allows citizens to own private property.

b. The government owns the resources and does not allow citizens to own private property.

c. Resources and private property are both owned by citizens.

d. Resources are owned by citizens, but not private property.

6. What is capital?

a. A measure of individual income.

b. The head of a company, also known as the CEO.

c. The resources needed to start or expand a business.

d. A meeting place for a company's board of directors.

7. What is inflation?

a. An expansion of business

b. An increase in the value of money

c. A decrease in the value of money

d. A growth in unemployment

8. A country's labor force excludes

a. employees that work as professionals

b. employees that are not union members

c. employees that are union members

d. children that are too young to work

9. Which of the following is a good example of a blue collar occupation?

a. Miner

b. Professor

c. Scientist

d. Accountant

10. What is consumer confidence?

a. The optimism held by the general public regarding the economy.

b. The trust that consumers have that the products they buy are safe.

c. The demand for a product.

d. The marketing used to make products seem valuable.

11. Unemployment figures do not include

a. white collar labor markets

b. former government employees

c. people who lost their jobs due to economic depression

d. retirees

12. Workers that are released from employment for temporary periods of time and brought back to the same jobs are said to be

    a. retired.

    b. laid off.

    c. fired.

    d. underemployed.

13. The federal government borrows money by

    a. delaying payments to employees.

    b. selling bonds.

    c. cutting off funding to certain programs.

    d. taxing citizens and corporations.

14. The federal government regulates

    a. gubernatorial elections.

    b. school curricula.

    c. state universities.

    d. interstate commerce.

15. The federal government can print more money to stimulate the economy, however this may cause

    a. deflation.

    b. stagflation.

    c. inflation.

    d. unemployment.

16. Classical economics holds that over time, economic problems will be corrected by the

    a. policies of the government.

    b. invisible hand of the market.

    c. people.

    d. raising of taxes.

17. A lack of money to fund a budget is called a

    a. deficit.

    b. savings.

    c. debt.

    d. loan

18. The federal government has carried significant amounts of debt since

    a. the Civil War.

    b. the 1980s.

    c. the Great Depression.

    d.the 2010s.

19. The value of all goods and services produced in a country is the

    a. per Capita Income.

    b. gross Domestic Product.

    c. net Exports.

    d. capital.

20. When a country chooses to spend time and resources making a product, it loses out on all of the other products it could have spent its time and resources making. This is known as

    a. a deficit.

    b. opportunity cost.

    c. economy of scale.

    d. gross domestic income.

Answer Key

Part 1 - World History

1. B
Combining copper and tin creates bronze.

Choice A is incorrect; there is no Tin Age.

Choice C is incorrect; The Stone Age came before The Bronze Age and is known for its use of stone, not metal.

Choice D is incorrect; The Iron Age came after The Bronze Age and is known for its use of iron.

2. A
The Punic Wars happened in Rome in the 3rd century BCE.

Choice B is incorrect; the Persian Wars happened in the 5th century BCE.

Choice C is incorrect; the Parthenon was constructed during the 5th century BCE.

Choice D is incorrect; Socrates lived in Greece during the 5th century BCE.

3. D
Democracy was first introduced in Athens in the 6th century.

Choice A is incorrect; dictatorships were first introduced in Rome in the 6th century.

Choice B is incorrect; Communism was first introduced in Russia in the 19th century.

Choice C is incorrect; Capitalism was first introduced in Europe in the MIddle Ages.

4. A
Ares, Aphrodite, Demeter and Athena are the names of four ancient Greek gods.

Choice B is incorrect; when Rome overtook Greece, they adopted some of their gods, but called them by different names.

Choices C is incorrect, Egyptian and Norse gods had different names.

5. C
Egypt attacking Rome at that time did not contribute to the fall of the Roman Empire. All the other choice were contributing factors.

Choice A is incorrect; the spread of Christianity displaced Roman religion.

Choice B is incorrect; Rome had grown very large and difficult to govern leading to civil war.

Choice D is incorrect; as Rome stopped expanding they were no longer gaining slaves and were unable to support themselves.

6. D
Vedas are ancient texts composed in Vedic Sandskrit.

Choice A is incorrect; this was not a time period in history.

Choice B is incorrect; this was not the name of the ruling class.

Choice C is incorrect; it is not known what happened to the Harappans, and the next invaders were the Aryans.

7. A
There is some doubt as to whether the Xia Dynasty existed, however, some recorded and archeological evidence that hints that it did.

Choice B is incorrect; the Han dynasty was a golden age in Chinese history where Imperial China started, but it was not

the first dynasty.
Choice C is incorrect; the Tang dynasty is another golden age of culture and society of Chinese history, Chang'an the capital of China was the largest city in the world at the time.

Choice D is incorrect; the Qing Dynasty was the last imperial dynasty of China, not the first.

8. D
Both Isaac Newton and Gottfried Leibniz discovered calculus independently - it was not invented by the Chinese.

The other choices are all inventions by the Chinese. Paper making was invented by the Chinese around 200 BCE, the Chinese first used chemical warfare during about 400 BCE, using the smoke of burnt mustard plants to kill their enemies, and the first use of gunpowder by the Chinese was before 1000 CE.

9. A
Buddhism maintains anyone can follow the Eightfold path to correct behavior and reach Nirvana.

Choice B is incorrect; in Hinduism, someone must go through a series of reincarnations before they can reach enlightenment.

Choice C is incorrect; Islam follows the teachings of the Qur'an.

Choice D is incorrect; Taoism is a Chinese philosophy of living.

10. B
Islam emerged in Arabia in 7th century CE. Some archaeologists prefer to use the terms Before the Common Era (B.C.E.) and the Common Era (C.E.), which are exactly the same as B.C. and A.D. but have nothing to do with Christianity.

Choice A is incorrect; Christianity emerged in Rome in 1st century CE.
Choice C is incorrect; Judaism emerged in Israel in 6th cen-

tury BCE.

Choice D is incorrect; Zoroastrianism emerged in Indo-Iran in 2nd century BCE.

11. B
A national language is not necessary to form a Nation.

Choice A is incorrect; breaking with the Catholic Church gave more power to the monarchy and increased nationalism in England.

Choice C is incorrect; Napoleon was influential in unifying France and caused other European nations to band together.

Choice D is incorrect; the creation of central governments caused laws and policy to be uniform across nations.

12. D
Following the fall of the Roman Empire, the Roman army was no longer supported by tax from the elite. Had this tax continued to support the Roman army, they could have stopped the inward migration.

Choice A is incorrect; Eastern Europe did not experience violence during this time.

Choice B is incorrect; rapid increases in population did not cause large scale migration.

Choice C is incorrect; the Roman Empire was not experiencing prosperity at that time.

13. C
The printing press is generally thought to be the most important invention of the Renaissance, and perhaps in the history of the world. Invented by German Johannes Gutenberg around 1440, the printing press made classical texts and other works available on a large scale, which influenced Renaissance thinking. By 1500 there were printing presses throughout Europe.
Choice A is incorrect; the steam engine was developed dur-

ing the Industrial Revolution.

Choice B is incorrect; the flying shuttle was developed during the Industrial Revolution.

Choice D is incorrect; although lenses were developed during the Renaissance, they were not a cause.

14. A
Thomas More was a Renaissance humanist who wrote about the Utopian political system in Utopia.

Choice B is incorrect; Niccolo Machiavelli was a Renaissance writer who wrote The Prince.

Choice C is incorrect; Martin Luther was a Renaissance Protestant leader who wrote the 95 theses attacking the Church.

Choice D is incorrect; Nicholas Copernicus was a Renaissance mathematician who developed the heliocentric view of the universe.

15. C
Although people increasingly looked to the monarchy to solve their problems, this was not a result of the Renaissance.

Choice A is incorrect; during the Renaissance the arts and sciences flourished.

Choice B is incorrect; the Church no longer possessed the unquestioned authority that it once had.

Choice D is incorrect; there was increased use of national languages such as English, Italian, and French.

16. B
An increased spirit of inquiry by the people, interference by the Pope in non-religious matters and selling of indulgences by the Church led to the Reformation, which was a loss of power for the Church and Pope.
Choice A is incorrect; the Renaissance was a time of intellec-

tual growth before the Reformation.

Choice C is incorrect; the Scientific Revolution was a time of advancement in the sciences following Reformation.

Choice D is incorrect; the Protestant Revolution was a Puritan rebellion in Maryland, though the Reformation is sometimes called the Protestant Reformation.

17. D
Following the Reformation, there was an increase in religious prosecution through the Spanish Inquisition, not an end to religious persecution.

Choice A is incorrect; Protestantism was formed during the Reformation.

Choice B is incorrect; The Thirty Years' War was a conflict between Catholics and Protestants following Reformation.

Choice C is incorrect; rulers had more power following the Reformation and did not need to listen to the Pope.

18. C
Martin Luther is most famous for pinning his 95 theses to a church door, which started the Reformation.

Choice A is incorrect; John Calvin's writings led to the formation of Presbyterian churches.

Choice B is incorrect; Martin Luther was not a priest and did not promote religious tolerance.

Choice D is incorrect; Thomas More wrote Utopia.

19. A
Johannes Kepler wrote the laws of planetary motion, which later influenced Isaac Newton.

Choice B is incorrect; Galileo was a scientist who invented the microscope and telescope.

Choice C is incorrect; Francis Bacon studied logic and ethics in science.

Choice D is incorrect; Rene Descartes was the inventor of deductive reasoning.

20. A
Nicholas Copernicus determined that the earth revolves around the sun.

Choice B is incorrect; Tycho Brahe believed that the sun moved around the earth and other planets moved around the sun.

Choice C is incorrect; Francis Bacon studied logic and ethics in science.

Choice D is incorrect; Isaac Newton studied universal laws of gravitation.

21. D
The need for military advancement did not lead to the Scientific Revolution.

Choice A is incorrect; expansion of trade led to scientific research for sea voyages.

Choice B is incorrect; humanism spread the idea that humans could accomplish anything.

Choice C is incorrect; the Reformation led to a loss of power for the Catholic Church, which had previously prevented scientific study.

22. B
Trading for spices, tea and silk in the Indies was the main reason for European exploration of Asia.

Choice A is incorrect; spreading Christianity was not an original goal of European explorers.

Choice C is incorrect; Europe was not reliant on slaves from Asia.
Choice D is incorrect; acquisition of land was not the main

reason for exploration of Asia.

23. D
Pollution was not a major result of colonization.

Choice A is incorrect; resources were removed from Africa and manufactured in Europe.

Choice B is incorrect; civil was not a result of colonization.

Choice C is incorrect; war, poor economy and famine caused by European powers led to poverty.

24. C
Europe was not afraid of Africa or Asia attacking.

Choice A is incorrect; following the Industrial Revolution there were many unemployed people who could be sent to live and work in colonies.

Choice B is incorrect; by forming colonies, Europe had access to a lot more resources.

Choice D is incorrect; many countries were competing to have the most colonies.

25. C
Spain and Portugal were the first European powers to colonize the Americas in the late 15th century.

Choice A is incorrect; England and France first colonized the Americas in the 16th century.

Choice B is incorrect; Spain was one of the first, but France was not.

Choice D is incorrect; Portugal was one of the first, but England was not.

26. B
Disease was a major cause of death as the Europeans brought diseases to the Americas that indigenous peoples had not encountered.

Choice A is incorrect; although warfare did cause deaths, it was not the leading cause.

Choice C and D are incorrect; starvation was not a leading cause of death among indigenous peoples.

27. A
Ancient Egyptian culture is divided into several periods, the middle of which is called the Middle Kingdom.

Choice B is incorrect because ancient Rome was reportedly founded in 753 BC.

Choice C is incorrect. Though the Chinese word for China translates to "Middle Kingdom," there is no Middle Kingdom period in ancient Chinese History.

Choice D is incorrect. Though ancient Sumerians did exist during this time period, they were not known as the Middle Kingdom.

28. B
Mesopotamia refers to the Tigris and Euphrates river system that housed many of the first written accounts of civilization circa 3100 BC.

Choice A is incorrect because Mesopotamia pre-dates Egypt.

Choice C is incorrect. Though India is geographically close, it is not a part of the Mesopotamian region.

Choice D is incorrect. Though China is known for early civilization, Mesopotamian civilization predates Chinese civilization.

29. C
Augustus ruled Rome from 27 BC to 14 AD.

Choice A is incorrect. Julius Caesar was never an emperor.

Choice B is incorrect because Claudius was the fourth emperor of Rome.

Choice D is incorrect because Nero was the fifth emperor of Rome.

30. D
The Qin dynasty marks the beginning of Imperial China at 221 BC.

Choice A is incorrect because the Qing dynasty was the last dynasty of Imperial China.

Choice B is incorrect because the Sui dynasty is in the middle of the era of Imperial China.

Choice C is incorrect because the Xia dynasty was a part of ancient China.

31. C
The Mandate of Heaven is the Chinese belief that heaven granted emperors the right to rule.

Choice A is incorrect. There is no such thing as the Mandate of God.

Choice B is incorrect. Though the Mandate does take place in China, the Mandate of China is incorrect.

Choice D is incorrect. There is no such thing as the Chinese Mandate.

32. B
Rome and Carthage fought each other.

Choice A is incorrect. Rome and Egypt never fought each other in the Punic Wars.

Choice C is incorrect. Egypt and Carthage never fought each other in the Punic Wars.

Choice D is incorrect. Choice B is the correct answer.
33. D
Charlemagne was the first Holy Roman Emperor.

Choice A is incorrect because Louis I was the second Holy Roman Emperor.
Choice B is incorrect because Charles II was the fifth Holy Roman Emperor.

Choice C is incorrect because Lothair I was the third Holy Roman Emperor.

34. C
Henry VIII was the father of Mary I.

Choice A is incorrect. Mary I was born in 1516. Henry V lived from 1386-1422.

Choice B is incorrect. Mary I was born in 1516. Henry VI lived from 1421-1471.

Choice D is incorrect. Mary I was born in 1516. Charles II wasn't born until 1630.

35. B
The French Revolution began in 1789.

Choice A is incorrect. The French Revolution wouldn't start until two years later.

Choice C is incorrect. 1790 is the year after the French Revolution began.

Choice D is incorrect. The French Revolution ended in 1799.

Part II - US History

1. D
The Foreign Trade Act did not take place until centuries after the American Revolutionary War. All the Intolerable Acts took place in the lead-up to the American Revolutionary War.

Choice A is incorrect; the Stamp Act imposed a tax on the colonies by forcing them to use paper produced in Britain for many printed materials. This was the first of the Intolerable Acts or taxes that were placed on British American subjects without their consent.

Choice B is incorrect; the Townshed Acts were also part of the Intolerable Acts that were meant to raise revenue in the colonies for the employment of judges and governors. These were also used to punish colonists and force compliance with the numerous other taxes being levied against the colonies.

Choice C is incorrect; the Tea Act allowed the British East India Company to sell tea directly to the colonies, thus making it cheaper. Many colonists hated this act because a small tax was added without their consent, which resulted in the Boston Tea Party.

2. B
The British imposed taxes through the Intolerable Acts either without representation from the colonies at all, or with representatives that effectively had no say in the matter.

Choice A is incorrect; even during the American Revolutionary War, most of the colonists did not decisively want to be free from British rule; they either wanted to stay under British rule, or were undecided.

Choice C is incorrect; while Colonists and people everywhere do not like to be taxed, most realized taxes were what allowed government to function and the colonists made no statements against ALL taxes, just some of them.

3. B
After the Seven Years War with France, Great Britain had a lot of debt and Parliament wanted the colonies to pay for some of the military expenditures and the cost of maintaining a military presence in the colonies.

Choice A is incorrect; None of the Intolerable Acts were used to raise revenue for the British Parliament salaries. The Intolerable Acts were used to pay off war debt, punish the colonies, and a variety of other things.

Choice C is incorrect; the Navigation Acts kept most trade in the British Colonies strictly between the colonies and Great Britain.

Choice D is incorrect; while the East India Company was fighting in India at this time, the British military was not involved there yet.

4. A
The Second Continental Congress tried to avert war even though the battles of Lexington and Concord had already been fought. This was known as the Olive Branch Petition. King James would not receive the petition because it came from what he perceived as an illegal and illegitimate assembly.

Choice C is false; because while Thomas Jefferson wrote the first draft of the petition, most of it was redrafted, and it was never called Jefferson's Plea.

Choice D is false; neither Samuel nor John Adams thought the Plea would help, and contributed nothing to the process. The plea was never called Adam's Plea.

5. A
The First continental Congress met to discuss various ways of getting rid of the Intolerable Acts and petition the King of England for a redress of grievances.

Choice B is incorrect; this is the purpose of the Second Continental Congress.

Choice C is incorrect; the federal government was set up with the Articles of Confederation.

Choice D is incorrect; all the "states" at this point were not states yet, instead they were colonies that firmly belonged to Great Britain.

6. D

While many other things were achieved, the main purpose of the Second Continental Congress was to establish a Continental Army.

Choice A is incorrect; the federal government was set up with the Articles of Confederation

Choice B is incorrect; Responding to the Intolerable Acts was the purpose of the First Continental Congress

Choice C is incorrect; asking for French aid was officially done after the Second Continental Congress was over, though Benjamin Franklin and others hinted at this possibility with many French officials.

7. B

With the Declaration of Independence, the colonies disavowed the rule of Great Britain, effectively announcing a state of war between the colonists and Great Britain.

Choice A is incorrect; the Articles of Confederation Established a federal government and occurred after there was a state of war between Great Britain and the Colonies.

Choice C is incorrect; the United States Constitution was a document that strengthened the federal government and, provided more effective ways of raising revenue.

Choice D is incorrect; while a declaration of hostilities does announce a state of war, there was no such document called the Declaration of Hostilities.

8. D

All the reasons listed were part of Manifest Destiny,

- Many Americans believed that they were special and could use the land better than anyone else.

- The agrarian ideal was a very popular idea at the time, many dreamed that America should be populated by self-sufficient farmers. With all the "open" land in the west this seemed like a real possibility.

- Many Americans believed that God had set America a destiny to bring civilization to the west, and that America would one day stretch across the continent.

9. A

The Clermont steamboat's maiden voyage between New York and Albany took 32 hours, much less time than the four days it would take the average sloop. This showed distances were shrinking time-wise.

Choice B is incorrect; while the Mexican American War brought many people west it was not the start of western expansion.

Choice C is incorrect; the invention of the telegraph greatly helped communication across the country, but it was not invented until long after western expansion had started.

Choice D is incorrect; gold in California brought more people west faster than ever before, but western expansion had already started decades before.

10. B

Gold was discovered in California in 1848, and the Gold Rush commenced.

Choice A is incorrect; while the miners were called 49ers after the year that most people started mining for gold in California, this was not when the Gold Rush started.

Choice C is incorrect; this was the year that the Gold Rush ended in California.

Choice D is incorrect; this was the year that California was admitted to the Union, not when the Gold Rush started.

11. A

The largest land acquisition, The Louisiana Purchase, was orchestrated under the Jefferson Administration and nearly doubled the size of the United States adding on almost 828,000 square miles.

Choice B is incorrect; the Treaty of Guadalupe Hidalgo added 525,000 sq miles to the United States and Mexico lost nearly half of their land. This was still a smaller land acquisition than the Louisiana Purchase.

Choice C is incorrect; the Texas Annexation incorporated the Republic of Texas into the United States and brought in about 390,000 square miles of land to the Union. This was also less than the Louisiana Purchase.

Choice D is incorrect; the Gadsden Purchase was the last time that the United States acquired land from Mexico with this $10 million purchase which added territory onto New Mexico and Arizona. This acquisition was for about 30,000 sqare miles which was less than the Louisiana Purchase.

12. D

Texas was an independent nation from about 1836 to 1845 with its own government and president. Mexico did not recognize its independence, but they were effectively independent until annexation by the United States in 1845.

Choice A is incorrect; Delaware was the first state in the Union in 1787, but was not created during westward expansion. Before being a state, it was a colony of Great Britain, not a sovereign nation.

Choice B is incorrect; California claimed to be an independent nation for less than a year, but never installed a civil administration or a president.

Choice C is incorrect; Alaska was a territory of Russia before becoming part of the Union, and never was a sovereign nation.

13. C
The Transcontinental Railroad greatly reduced the time it took to travel across the United States from almost half a year to about a week.

Choice A is incorrect; the telegraph was the fastest way for information (not people) to travel across the Continental United States.

Choice B is incorrect; the Clearmont steamboat marked the start of westward expansion, but it did not provide the shortest trip across the United States.

Choice D is incorrect; the Northwest Passage is a sea route that runs through the Arctic Ocean from the tips of Russia and Alaska, above Canada, and into the Atlantic Ocean. It was first discovered in 1903, but remained closed for most of each year until about 2010. This passage was dangerous and never a significant part of western expansion.

14. A
With Arizona's statehood in 1912, all the west to the Pacific ocean was incorporated into the United States.

Choice B is incorrect; the end of the Mexican American War in 1848 was more than half a century before the end of western expansion.

Choice C is incorrect; there is no such thing as the Completion Speech.

Choice D is incorrect; President William Mckinley's Assassination in 1901 did not have an effect on westward expansion.

15. C
Many Native Americans were forcefully relocated out of the Deep South if they failed to assimilate. This occurred during much of the 1830s. Most deaths occurred near the end when the army detained many Native Americans who had not left and forced them west, many died due to disease, exposure and starvation.

Choice A is incorrect; the Trail of Tears occurred before the United States military and the various Sioux tribes were at war.

Choice B is incorrect; Irish immigrants were never forcefully removed en mass from New York

Choice D is incorrect; while the Transcontinental Railroad claimed many lives in its construction no part of it was ever called the Trail of Tears.

16. A
Democrat President Jackson and his supporters believed that all white males, the common man, should have the right to vote, and not just those that owned property or paid certain taxes.

Choice B is incorrect; almost no one believed minorities should be able to vote.

Choice C is incorrect; women were not directly part of the political process and the belief that women were too "fragile" or emotional for the process would hold sway after the Jacksonian Democrats were no longer a political party.

Choice D is incorrect; Jacksonian Democrats were explicitly against the landed gentry having all the political power.

17. C
The Second Great Awakening was a movement that rejected skepticism and rationalism. The supporters called for everyone to become more moral and less analytical.

Choice A is incorrect; while it was a multi-denominational religious movement, people believed the second coming of Christ was imminent, which would be followed by a thousand years of peace, not the end of the world.
Choice B is incorrect; the Second Great Awakening was a religious movement that emphasized faith over logic.

Choice D is incorrect; while reducing corruption in politics may have been part of the increase in morality the Second Great Awakening called for, the movement was religious, and not about corruption in politics.

18. B
With Marbury v. Madison, Chief Justice Marshall allowed Marshall to establish the concept of judicial review. Judicial review is the concept that only the supreme court can declare a law unconstitutional, and is the sole power of the Supreme Court.

Choice A is incorrect; Fletcher v. Peck in 1810 was the first ruling that ruled a state law was unconstitutional. This enlarged the powers of the supreme court, but not as much as Marbury v. Madison.

Choice C is incorrect; Brown vs. Board of Education declared that segregated schools were unconstitutional. The ruling had no effect on the powers of the Supreme Court and was not presided over by Chief Justice Marshall.

Choice D is incorrect; Roe vs. Wade dealt with when women could get abortions. This did not have an effect on the Supreme Court's power, nor did Chief Justice Marshall preside over the court that decided that case.

19. D
While the Lewis and Clark expedition did try to establish some American presence in unclaimed territory on the West Coast, they did not try to claim any of the Spanish territory on the border of the Louisiana Purchase.

Choice A is incorrect; exploring and mapping the Louisiana Purchase was a chief reason that the expedition was funded.

Choice B is incorrect; President Jefferson's main purpose for the expedition was to find a water route across the continent for future commerce.

Choice C is incorrect; the United States did want to establish a presence in the Louisiana Territory to strengthen their claim.

20. B
The First Barbary War was the first war on a foreign soil

authorized by congress.

Choice A is incorrect; many European powers paid tribute to the Barbary States to ensure that their trading ships were not harassed.

Choice C is incorrect; Spain suggested the United States should pay the tribute to prevent further attacks after the Spanish negotiated for the release of the captured ship and crew.

Choice D is incorrect; while the United States was winning some strategic battles, a treaty was drawn up in which there would be an end to hostilities and a complete prisoner exchange, with the United States paying an additional ransom for the extra prisoners Tripoli had.

21. C
The Monroe Doctrine was proclaimed under President James Monroe that the United States would view any influence or colony-making in the Americas as an act of war. In addition, the United States would stay out of European affairs.

Choice A is incorrect; while suffrage for all white males happened in the 1820s when the Monroe Doctrine was established, it was not the same thing.

Choice B is incorrect; the removal of Native Americans from the Deep South was started under the Indian Removal Act, not the Monroe Doctrine.

Choice D is incorrect; the Roosevelt Corollary states that the United States would be the police of the Americas, and expand their influence throughout the Americas also.

22. A
West Virginia split off from Virginia to stay in the Union and avoid joining the rest of Virginia in the Confederacy.

Choice B is incorrect; while Tennessee was not part of the original Confederate States of America, it joined later, when war was imminent.

Choice C is incorrect; Texas was an original signatory to the Confederate Constitution.

Choice D is incorrect; Florida was also one of the original signatories to the Confederate Constitution.

23. B
The North and the South had very different economies that did not compete. Unfortunately, both had very different wants when it came to commercial laws.

Choice A is incorrect; the right to own slaves was a belief that the Southern States held strongly, and they believed the North seemed to be impinging on that right at every opportunity. With the addition of new states, and whether they be slave or free, this issue became more and more heated.

Choice C is incorrect; the Southern States believed that each state could leave the Union if they wanted, and that state laws covered their citizens even in other states. The Northern states disagreed, believing states could not leave the union and citizens could not take slaves into a free state.

Choice D is incorrect; the Southern States wanted tariffs against foreign cotton and not on manufactured goods, while the North wanted the opposite. Usually the North got its way, angering the South.

24. D
The Missouri Compromise was an effort by Congress to defuse the sectional and political rivalries triggered by the request of Missouri late in 1819 for admission as a state in which slavery would be permitted. All areas of the Louisiana Territory north of 36°30', except for Missouri, would enter the union as free states

Choice A is incorrect; Missouri entered the Union as a slave state in accordance with the Missouri Compromise, but Texas did not enter as a free state.

Choice B is incorrect; Missouri entered the Union as a slave state in accordance with the Missouri Compromise.

Choice C is incorrect; California was not part of the Missouri Compromise.

25. D

The Kansas–Nebraska Act of 1854 (10 Stat. 277) created the territories of Kansas and Nebraska, opening new lands for settlement, and had the effect of repealing the Missouri Compromise of 1820 by allowing white male settlers in those territories to determine through popular sovereignty whether they would allow slavery within each territory.

There was to be a vote by the white males who lived in Kansas and Nebraska on whether to be slave or slave-free states. This did not work very well in Kansas due to many people who lived outside the state returning to vote. Violence ensued which has been called the bleeding of Kansas.

Choice A is incorrect; the Kansas-Nebraska Act did not have a decisive ruling on whether either Nebraska or Kansas would be slave or free states.

Choice B is incorrect; the Kansas-Nebraska Act was only about Kansas and Nebraska and did not concern any other part of the former Louisiana Territories.

Choice C is incorrect; this is the Missouri Act except for Kansas and Nebraska have replaced Missouri, not the Kansas-Nebraska Act.

26. C

Many southern states vowed to secede from the Union if Lincoln was elected to presidency, and they followed through with their threat, forming the Confederate States of America, or the Confederacy.

Choice A is incorrect; the Emancipation Proclamation happened well into the Civil War.
Choice B is incorrect; while Jefferson Davis may have vowed that the South would no longer bend to the will of the North, this did not lead to the Confederacy.

Choice D is incorrect; Robert E. Lee never wanted the Civil War to happen, but his loyalties lay with Virginia and so he fought for the Confederacy.

27. C
The Confederate States believe Europe would side with them, as the South grew most of the cotton that fueled the European textile industries. This did not happen because the cotton output of the South had been so high for so long, Europe had amassed huge stockpiles, and other suppliers such as India picked up the production slack.

Choice A is incorrect; while the North had large tariffs to support its industries, this was common practice in Europe and never thought to be a big factor in deciding who the Europeans might support.

Choice B is incorrect; while many of the upper class in the South had family in Europe, so did many in the Union. This was one reason Europe stayed mostly neutral in the war.

Choice D is incorrect; the Europeans were actually more likely to identify with the North over the issue of slavery, which had been outlawed in Europe for some time.

28. B
The Confederate attack on Fort Sumter was in effect a declaration of war and the opening volley of the American Civil War.

Choice A is incorrect; Abraham Lincoln's election was the justification for the formation of the Confederate States of America, but it did not start the war.

Choice C is incorrect; the Battle of Gettysburg was the bloodiest battle of the Civil War, the war had already begun.

Choice D is incorrect; the Battle of Antietam was the first major battle on Union soil, but the war had already begun.

29. A
European immigrants were the biggest labor base in the Second Industrial Revolution.

Choice B is incorrect; while children were a part of the

workforce, and endured many hardships during the Second Industrial Revolution, they were not the largest labor base. Choice C is incorrect; Mexican immigrants were very uncommon during the Second Industrial Revolution.

Choice D is incorrect; during the Second Industrial Revolution slavery was outlawed.

30. C
The United States did not grow rubber and it did not play a large part in the United States becoming an industrial nation during the late 19th century.

Choice A is incorrect; oil was very helpful with lighting and a variety of other purposes allowing the United States to become a major industrial nation.

Choice B is incorrect; wood was an essential natural resource that supplied the raw building materials needed for the United States to become a major industrial nation.

Choice D is incorrect; there is a large deposits of coal found in the United States. Coal, like oil, helped fuel the United states into becoming a major industrial nation in the late 19th century.

31. A
Choice A is correct, highways did not come into being until the 20th century.

Choice B is incorrect; steel manufacturing was very important in that it was stronger than the alternative metal of the day, wrought iron. It could support and pull heavier loads, allowing for bigger buildings, stronger railroads, etc.

Choice C is incorrect; railroads were essential for the movement of commerce, especially larger things that could not be pulled by horses, or transported by boat.

Choice D is incorrect; the telegraph sped up communication, allowing supply to meet demand more readily.

32. C

Many countries experienced the Second Industrial Revolution.

Choice A is incorrect; most industrial works saw a large increase in incomes.

Choice B is incorrect; the United States had high domestic tariffs.

Choice D is incorrect; the telegraph was invented before the Second Industrial Revolution occurred.

33. D
Samuel Gompers was deeply involved with unions, fighting for the rights of workers, making him almost the opposite of a Robber Baron.

Choice A is incorrect; John Rockefeller was a major promoter of capitalism and had a huge stake in oil, making him a Robber Baron.

Choice B is incorrect; J.P. Morgan was the largest banker of the period, making him a Robber Baron.

Choice C is incorrect; Andrew Carnegie was a huge industrialist in the steel industry of the time, also making him a Robber Baron.

34. A
The National Labor Union was the first national labor union, though it was only marginally successful in its goals.

Choice B is incorrect; the Federation of Organized Trades and Labor Unions was more successful than the National Labor Union, but came later.

Choice C is incorrect; the Knights of Labor was the first effective national labor union, but it was not the first one.

Choice D is incorrect; the American Federation of labor came into being after the National Labor Union, and was the first national federation of labor unions, but not the first national labor union.

35. B

The United States declared war on Japan after Japan bombed Pearl Harbor.

Choice A is incorrect, the United States did not enter WWII to support France.

Choice C is incorrect, the United States was not allied with Great Britain.

Choice D is incorrect, that is not why the United States entered WWII.

Part III - Geography

1. C

Open spaces is not a reason that humans move to urban areas.

Choice A is incorrect; people move to cities for excitement.

Choice B is incorrect; most universities are located in cities.

Choice D is incorrect; cities normally have more job opportunities than rural areas.

2. B

The era of human existence before writing was developed is known as prehistory.

Choices A and B are incorrect; ancient and recorded history are written.

Choice D is incorrect; unknown history is not a real term.

3. C

A thin stretch of land that connects two large areas of land is called an isthmus.

4. B

An ecosystem is a group of living organisms and their surrounding environment.
All the other choices are incorrect, but plausible, due to the

eco- prefix.

5. B
The Indian ocean borders the east coast of Africa.

Choice A is incorrect; the Atlantic borders the west coast.

Choices C and D are clearly incorrect; the pacific doesn't border Africa.

6. A
Cuba, Haiti and Puerto Rico are located in the Caribbean Sea.

Choice B is incorrect; the North Sea borders Europe.

Choice C is incorrect; the Indian Ocean borders Asia and Africa.

Choice D is incorrect; the Black Sea is adjacent to the Mediterranean.

7. D
The Ural Mountains separate the continents of Europe and Asia.
Choice A is incorrect; North and South America are not separated by mountains.

Choice B is incorrect; Africa and Asia are not separated by mountains.

Choice C is incorrect; Australia is an island.

8. A
Australia is a continent, though not a large one.

Continents have the following characteristics:

- Areas of geologically stable continental crust, or cratons, tectonically independent from other continents
- Biological distinctiveness, with unique animal and plant life

- Cultural uniqueness
- Local belief in separate continental status

9. A

A nation is also known as a country; nation and country are interchangeable terms.

Choice B is incorrect; although nations have governments, they are not interchangeable.

Choice C is incorrect; a society does not have to be a nation.

Choice D is clearly incorrect; a utopia is a fictional place.

10. D

Physical maps show features such as mountains, lakes and rivers.

Choice A is incorrect; a political map shows borders of countries.

Choice B is incorrect; movements of populations are not shown on a physical map.

Choice C is incorrect; ruins are not shown on a physical map.

11. A

Country borders are a feature shown most clearly on a political map.

Choice B is incorrect; movements of populations are not shown on a political map.

Choice C is incorrect; ruins are not shown on a political map.

Choice D is incorrect; a physical map shows features such as mountains, lakes and rivers.

12. C

Anthropology is the study of human movements and the development of society.

Choice A is incorrect; biology is the study of organic life.

Choice B is incorrect; archeology is the study of artifacts.

Choice D is incorrect; paleontology is the study of fossils.

13. B
The study of the artifacts is known as archaeology.

Choice A is incorrect; biology is the study of how life works.

Choice C is incorrect; anthropology is the study of human movements and the development of society.

Choice D is incorrect; paleontology is the study of fossils.

14. D
The connection of different societies through technology such as the telephone, cellular phone and internet is known as the communications revolution.

Choice A and C are incorrect; agriculture has little to do with this.

Choice B is incorrect; the industrial revolution came earlier.

15. B
Globalization refers to the connection of all the economies in the world.

Choice A is incorrect; globalization refers to economics, not education.

Choice C is incorrect; although plausible due to the large colonial territories it refers to.

Choice D is incorrect; the study of ancient civilizations is archeology.

16. C
The summit is the top of a mountain.

Choice A is incorrect. Though the apex is often considered

the point of something, it is not the top of a mountain.

Choice B is incorrect. The crown can also be known as the top of something, but it is not the top of a mountain.

Choice D is incorrect. The peak is a point of a mountain. The summit is the highest peak.

17. A
Total population divided by total area equals population density.

Choice B is incorrect. Total population multiplied by total area does not give you population density.

Choice C is incorrect. Population density is not calculated this way.

Choice D is incorrect. Population density is not calculated this way.

18. A
The internet connects billions of people instantaneously.

Choice B is incorrect. The telegraph sped up communication in the 19th century.

Choice C is incorrect. The telephone was the best method of diffusion before the internet.

Choice D is incorrect. Sending a letter takes a long time and is not conducive to instantaneous diffusion.

19. C
Functional regions are often identified by man-made borders.
Choice A is incorrect. Formal regions are regions connected by traits like a common language.

Choice B is incorrect. Territories are usually defined as a countries under the control of other countries.

Choice D is incorrect. Perceptual regions might refer to regions that people believe they belong in.

20. A
Language helps us identify formal regions.

Choice B is incorrect. Territories are usually defined as countries under the control of other countries.

Choice C is incorrect. Functional regions are identified by man-made borders.

Choice D is incorrect. Perceptual regions might refer to regions that people believe they belong in.

Part IV - Social Studies Skills and Concepts

1. B
Belief systems are the established ways groups of people look at philosophical views and religious faith.

Choice A is incorrect. Conflict is a clash of ideas from incompatible forces.

Choice C is incorrect. Change is trying to evoke an alteration in ideas or events.

Choice D is incorrect. Culture is patterns of human behavior (ideas, beliefs, values, etc.) that are transmitted to succeeding generations.

2. A
Interdependence is defined as relying on others in mutually beneficial ways.

Choice B is incorrect. Empathy is your ability to understand others because you're able to share their feelings.

Choice C is incorrect. Identity is your own unique values and attitudes.

Choice D is incorrect. Choice is your right to select from many alternatives

3. C
Justice is upheld when individuals are given fair treatment in personal, societal, and governmental interactions.

Choice A is incorrect; Power is your ability to influence the actions of others.

Choice B is incorrect; Empathy is your ability to understand others because you're able to share their feelings.

Choice D is incorrect; Citizenship happens when a country gives a person a recognized status under the law

4. B
Human rights are the basic political, social, and economic rights that all human are entitled to.

Choice A is incorrect; Laws are the rules governing the region you are in.

Choice C is incorrect; Justice happens when individuals are given fair treatment in personal, societal, and governmental interactions.

Choice D is incorrect; Values are the principles by which you live your life.

5. C
Civic Values are the principles that serve as the foundation for the United States' form of government.

Choice A is incorrect; Justice happens when individuals are given fair treatment in personal, societal, and governmental interactions.

Choice B is incorrect; Citizenship happens when a country

gives a person a recognized status under the law.

Choice D is incorrect; Decision Making is that process that we use to influence the many facets of our lives.

6. A
Decision Making is that process that we use to influence the many facets of our lives.

Choice B is incorrect; Rule breaking is not an official term, but refers to the time when a person breaks a rule or law.

Choice C is incorrect; Rationalizing is not an official term, but refers to the idea of a person trying to justify their actions by equating them with actions that are more acceptable.

Choice D is incorrect; Diversifying is an economic term used to describe a portfolio that is invested in many areas.

7. D
A politically organized society is run by a government.

Choice A is incorrect; A dictatorship is a form of government run by the absolute authority of a dictator.

Choice B is incorrect; An oligarchy is form of government run by a small group of people.

Choice C is incorrect; A monarchy is a form of government where sovereignty is embodied in one person.

8. B
Power is your ability to influence the actions of others.

Choice A is incorrect; Citizenship happens when a country gives a person a recognized status under the law.

Choice C is incorrect; Influence is similar to power, but it focuses more on character rather than actions.
Choice D is incorrect; Empathy is your ability to understand

others because you're able to share their feelings.

9. A
Monarchies, oligarchies, dictatorships, democracies, and republics are all political systems.

Choice B is incorrect; Though some forms of government are perceived as negative, all of them are not.

Choice C is incorrect; Though some forms of government are perceived as positive, all of them are not.

Choice D is incorrect; Though some forms of government are perceived as effective, all of them are not.

10. C
Voting fulfills one of the responsibility of citizenship.

Choice A is incorrect; Justice happens when individuals are given fair treatment in personal, societal, and governmental interactions.

Choice B is incorrect; Rights are the legal principles of freedom for individuals.

Choice D is incorrect; Voting does not allow people to rule the United States.

11. D
People are united by a geographic location or by a political organization are a part of the same nation-sate.
Choice A is incorrect; A dictatorial state is run by a dictator.

Choice B is incorrect; A democratic state is governed by the people.

Choice C is incorrect; A republican state is ruled by elected leaders, where the power resides in the people.

12. A
The conflict between our unlimited needs and how many
natural resources there are is called scarcity.

Choice B is incorrect; Depletion is the reduction in the
quantity of a certain thing.

Choice C is incorrect; Destruction is the act of causing
damage to something so that it no longer exists.

Choice D is incorrect; Expenditure is the act of spending.

13. B
An environment is defined as the natural and manmade
elements that surround us.

Choice A is incorrect; A location is simply a place.

Choice C is incorrect; Geography is the study of the earth's
surface.

Choice D is incorrect; Social Studies is the study of history,
geography, economics, government, etc.

14. A
The study of human activity on earth is called Human
Systems.

Choice B is incorrect; The study of human activity on earth
is called Human Systems.

Choice C is incorrect; Globalism is the attitude that places
the interests of the world over those of individual countries.

Choice D is incorrect; The study of human activity on earth
is called Human Systems.

15. C
Physical systems are the processes that shape Earth's
surface.

Choice A is incorrect; Geography is the study of the earth's surface.

Choice B is incorrect; The study of human activity on earth is called Human Systems.

Choice D is incorrect; Ecology is a branch of biology that focuses on the relationships of organisms to their surroundings.

Part V - Economics

1. A
As demand increases, supply tends to decrease.

Choice B is incorrect; supply and demand tend to be inversely related.

Choice C is clearly incorrect; demand has a strong influence on supply.

Choice D is incorrect; demand has a predictable effect on supply.

2. B
As supply increases, prices tend to decrease.

Choice A is incorrect; more supply lowers prices

Choices C and D are incorrect; supply has a predictable effect on prices.

3. A
As economies of scale increase, products are expensive to make at first, but eventually become less expensive to make. This usually applies to large items, such as airplanes and cars.

Choice B is incorrect; the opposite is true.

Choice C is incorrect; here products are not customized to individual customers.

Choice D is incorrect; bidding is irrelevant to production.

4. C
In a free market economy, citizens own resources and private property.

Choices A and D are incorrect by definition.

Choice B is the definition of a command economy.

5. B
In a command economy, the government owns the resources and does not allow citizens to own private property.

Choices A and D are incorrect by definition.

Choice C is incorrect; this is the definition of a free market economy.

6. C
Capital is the resource (namely money) needed to start or expand a business.

Choice A is incorrect; per capita income is a measure of individual income.

Choices B and D are incorrect but may sound plausible.

7. C
An increase in the value of money, or more precisely, a general increase in prices and fall in the purchasing value of money.
Choice A is incorrect; inflation refers to currency, not business.

Choice B is incorrect; this is the definition of deflation.

Choice D is incorrect; unemployment is not a cause of inflation.

8. D
A country's labor force excludes children who are too young to work and are not calculated as part of the job market.

Choice A is incorrect; professionals are included.

Choices B and C are incorrect but the word "labor" makes them seem plausible.

9. A
A miner is a physical laborer and a good example of a blue collar occupation.

Choices B, C and D are incorrect; a professor, a scientist and an accountant are all professionals.

10. A
Consumer confidence is an economic indicator which measures the degree of optimism consumers feel about the overall state of the economy and their personal financial situation.

Choices B and C are incorrect but sound plausible.

11. D
Unemployment figures do not include retirees, who are not expected to work.
Choice A is incorrect; white collar workers are an important part of unemployment statistics.

Choice B is incorrect; government employees are an important part of unemployment statistics.

Choice C is incorrect; economic depression affects unemployment figures greatly.
12. B
Workers that are released from employment for temporary periods of time and brought back to the same jobs are said to be laid off.

Choice A is incorrect; retired people are not expected to return to work.

Choice C is incorrect; fired workers do not expect to return to the same position.

Choice D is incorrect; underemployed workers simply want more hours to work.

13. B
The federal government borrows money by selling bonds. Bonds are loans to the government by the bond-holders.

Choices A and C are incorrect; delaying payments to employees, or cutting off funding do not amount to borrowing money.

Choice D is incorrect; taxing citizens and corporations is how the government gets its revenue.

14. D
The federal government regulates interstate commerce.

Choices A, B and C are incorrect; gubernatorial elections, school curricula, and state universities are a state and local matter.

15. C
The federal government can print money to stimulate the economy, however, increasing the money supply decreases the value of money and causes inflation.

Choice A is incorrect; deflation is an increase in the value of money.

Choice B is incorrect; stagflation is a possibility, but does not normally take place.

Choice D is incorrect; stagnation is a stalling of the economy, while increasing the money supply stimulates the economy.

16. B
Classical economics holds that over time, economic problems will be corrected by the invisible hand of the market. Adam Smith's theory of the invisible hand is an important part of classical economics.

Choice A is incorrect; classical economics was a free market school of thought.

Choice C is incorrect; the people's role in classical economics is simply to be consumers of goods produced.

Choice D is incorrect; classical economists would virtually never recommend raising taxes.

17. A
A lack of money to fund a budget is called a deficit.

Choice B is incorrect; a lack of money does not amount to a savings.

Choices C and D are incorrect; a debt, or a loan is money borrowed to cover deficits.

18. B
The federal government has carried significant amounts of debt since the 1980s, when it became normal for the U.S. to borrow more and more money each year to cover deficits.

Choice A is incorrect; the Civil War required borrowing, but the debts were not carried for long and paid off.

Choice C is incorrect; the Great Depression created debt, but the debts were paid off by the end of the 1940s.
Choice D is incorrect; 2010 was not the beginning of the practice of carrying large amounts of debt.

19. B
The value of all goods and services produced within a country is the Gross Domestic Product, or GDP.

Choice A is incorrect; per capita income is a measure of individual income.

Choice C is incorrect; net exports are only part of GDP.

Choice D is incorrect; capital is money and resources used to expand a business.

20. B
When a country chooses to spend time and resources making one product, it forgoes the other products it could have spent its time and resources making. This is known as opportunity cost.

Choice A is incorrect; a deficit is a budget shortage.

Choice C is incorrect; an economy of scale is not particularly related to opportunity cost.

Choice D is incorrect; gross domestic income is the total income brought into the economy.

Practice Test Questions Set 2

The questions below are not the same as you will find on the NMTA History, Geography, Economics, Civics and Government test- that would be too easy! And nobody knows what the questions will be and they change all the time. **Below are general questions that cover the same subject areas as the NMTA test and are intended for skill practice only.** So, while the format and exact wording of the questions may differ slightly, and change from year to year, if you can answer the questions below, you will have no problem with the NMTA test.

For the best results, take these Practice Test Questions as if it were the real exam. Set aside time when you will not be disturbed, and a location that is quiet and free of distractions. Read the instructions carefully, read each question carefully, and answer to the best of your ability.
Use the bubble answer sheets provided. When you have completed the Practice Questions, check your answer against the Answer Key and read the explanation provided.

Do not attempt more than one set of practice test questions in one day. After completing the first practice test, wait two or three days before attempting the second set of questions.

World History Answer Sheet

	A	B	C	D	E			A	B	C	D	E
1	○	○	○	○	○		21	○	○	○	○	○
2	○	○	○	○	○		22	○	○	○	○	○
3	○	○	○	○	○		23	○	○	○	○	○
4	○	○	○	○	○		24	○	○	○	○	○
5	○	○	○	○	○		25	○	○	○	○	○
6	○	○	○	○	○		26	○	○	○	○	○
7	○	○	○	○	○		27	○	○	○	○	○
8	○	○	○	○	○		28	○	○	○	○	○
9	○	○	○	○	○		29	○	○	○	○	○
10	○	○	○	○	○		30	○	○	○	○	○
11	○	○	○	○	○		31	○	○	○	○	○
12	○	○	○	○	○		32	○	○	○	○	○
13	○	○	○	○	○		33	○	○	○	○	○
14	○	○	○	○	○		34	○	○	○	○	○
15	○	○	○	○	○		35	○	○	○	○	○
16	○	○	○	○	○							
17	○	○	○	○	○							
18	○	○	○	○	○							
19	○	○	○	○	○							
20	○	○	○	○	○							

US History Answer Sheet

	A	B	C	D	E		A	B	C	D	E
1	○	○	○	○	○	21	○	○	○	○	○
2	○	○	○	○	○	22	○	○	○	○	○
3	○	○	○	○	○	23	○	○	○	○	○
4	○	○	○	○	○	24	○	○	○	○	○
5	○	○	○	○	○	25	○	○	○	○	○
6	○	○	○	○	○	26	○	○	○	○	○
7	○	○	○	○	○	27	○	○	○	○	○
8	○	○	○	○	○	28	○	○	○	○	○
9	○	○	○	○	○	29	○	○	○	○	○
10	○	○	○	○	○	30	○	○	○	○	○
11	○	○	○	○	○	31	○	○	○	○	○
12	○	○	○	○	○	32	○	○	○	○	○
13	○	○	○	○	○	33	○	○	○	○	○
14	○	○	○	○	○	34	○	○	○	○	○
15	○	○	○	○	○	35	○	○	○	○	○
16	○	○	○	○	○						
17	○	○	○	○	○						
18	○	○	○	○	○						
19	○	○	○	○	○						
20	○	○	○	○	○						

Geography Answer Sheet

	A	B	C	D
1	○	○	○	○
2	○	○	○	○
3	○	○	○	○
4	○	○	○	○
5	○	○	○	○
6	○	○	○	○
7	○	○	○	○
8	○	○	○	○
9	○	○	○	○
10	○	○	○	○
11	○	○	○	○
12	○	○	○	○
13	○	○	○	○
14	○	○	○	○
15	○	○	○	○
16	○	○	○	○
17	○	○	○	○
18	○	○	○	○
19	○	○	○	○
20	○	○	○	○

Social Science Answer Sheet

	A	B	C	D
1	○	○	○	○
2	○	○	○	○
3	○	○	○	○
4	○	○	○	○
5	○	○	○	○
6	○	○	○	○
7	○	○	○	○
8	○	○	○	○
9	○	○	○	○
10	○	○	○	○
11	○	○	○	○
12	○	○	○	○
13	○	○	○	○
14	○	○	○	○
15	○	○	○	○

Economics Answer Sheet

	A	B	C	D
1	○	○	○	○
2	○	○	○	○
3	○	○	○	○
4	○	○	○	○
5	○	○	○	○
6	○	○	○	○
7	○	○	○	○
8	○	○	○	○
9	○	○	○	○
10	○	○	○	○
11	○	○	○	○
12	○	○	○	○
13	○	○	○	○
14	○	○	○	○
15	○	○	○	○
16	○	○	○	○
17	○	○	○	○
18	○	○	○	○
19	○	○	○	○
20	○	○	○	○

Part I - US History

1. Why was the "Gilded Age" called the Gilded Age?

a. the California Gold Rush happened at that time

b. Gold was the major status symbol at the time

c. There was a class of super-rich who enjoyed a lavish life-style, while there were many in extreme poverty

d. Gangsters would gild enemies that were rich or greedy

2. What was the "Great Migration" of the United states in the early 1900s and late 1800s?

a. Many blacks moving out of the South

b. Large groups of European immigrants moving to the East Coast of the United States through Ellis Island

c. Asians immigrating to the West Coast of the United States

d. The last large movement of Native Americans to reservations

3. What created woman's suffrage in the United States?

a. The Seneca Falls Convention

b. The 18th Amendment

c. The 19th Amendment

d. The Jeannette Rankin Law

4. Who built the Panama Canal?

a. The French

b. The United States

c. The Spanish

d. Both A and B

5. What was the Open Door Policy?

a. All countries would lower tariffs for more open markets

b. Anyone could propose an idea to the president through the mail

c. China would be open to trade with all countries

d. A name coined for how people would go from government positions to being employed by the companies that lobbied them when they retired

6. What did the Federal Reserve Act do?

a. Gave legal authority to issue U.S. Dollars

b. Set up a government bank

c. All banks had to keep at least 10% of their capital liquid

d. Took United States assets out of private hands and put it in public trusts

7. What contributed to the United States joining World War I?

a. The bombing of Pearl Harbor

b. Alliances with Britain and France

c. German U-boats torpedoing United States ships

d. Both B and C

8. What did the Dawes Plan do?

a. Gave aid in the form of tools and materials to Europe for reconstruction

b. Gave money to Germany to pay war reparations to the Allies

c. Facilitated the immigration of displaced persons at the end of World War I to the United States in exchange for a certain amount of low paid labor

d. Gave money to countries who promised to fight communism

9. What was the start of the Great Depression?

a. Prohibition

b. The stock market collapse of 1929

c. Germany defaulting on its loans to the United States after World War I

d. The Dust Bowl

10. What did World War II unquestionably do for the Economy?

a. End the Great Depression

b. Reduce unemployment

c. Exacerbate the Great Depression

d. Choices A and B are still up to debate

11. What caused the Great Depression?

a. Excessive borrowing

b. Restricting the amount of money in the economy

c. People not spending money

d. All of the above

12. What caused the global trade to collapse during the Great Depression?

a. Smoot-Hawley Tariff Act

b. Revolutions in many developing nations

c. Black Tuesday

d. The Nazis and similar fascist groups taking power in many countries

13. Which one of these did President Roosevelt NOT implement to help end the Great Depression?

   a. Federally insure banks

   b. Social Security

   c. Pay people back who lost their bank accounts in the crash

   d. Repeal prohibition

14. Which of these did NOT end during the Great Depression?

   a Adherence to the Gold Standard

   b. Prohibition

   c. The Dust Bowl

   d. Tennessee Valley Authority

15. What were Roosevelt's "Fireside Chats?"

   a. Radio addresses to the nation explaining what he was doing

   b. Thirty talks with different world leaders to try and lessen the effects of the Great Depression

   c. Shows that Roosevelt put on for the newly invented television that endeared him to the nation

   d. Secret talks with key members of industry to try and reinvigorate the economy

16. Why did the United States enter the Pacific War in World War II?

   a. They were asked by France for support

   b. The Japanese bombed Pearl Harbor

   c. Germany declared War on Great Britain, whom the United States was allied to

   d. They felt morally compelled to fight against Germany

17. Which two Japanese cities did the United States bomb during World War II?

a. Hiroshima and Osaka

b. Nagasaki and Hokkaido

c. Hokkaido and Osaka

d. Hiroshima and Nagasaki

18. Who was the United States president during World War II?

a. Woodrow Wilson

b. Herbert Hoover

c. Harry Truman

d. Franklin Roosevelt

19. What did Rosie the Riveter encourage women to do during World War II?

a. To work in factories

b. To join the military

c. To support men in the workplace and military

d. To work producing food

20. What was one reason the Allied forces triumphed over the Axis powers in World War II?

a. The Allied forces were more organized

b. The Allied forces produced more supplies

c. The Allied forces new all the Axis powers plans in advance

d. The Allied forces were more technologically advanced

21. What did Executive Order 9066 do?

a. It allowed African Americans to join the military during WWII

b. It allowed women to join the military during WWII

c. It allowed Jews to immigrate into the United States during WWII

d. It allowed Japanese Americans to be placed in internment camps during WWII

22. Who ended the Cold War?

a. Ronald Reagan

b. Mikhail Gorbachev

c. John Kennedy

d. Nikita Khrushchev

23. What/who ended Détente?

a. Nikita Khrushchev

b. Invasion of Afghanistan

c. Invasion of Vietnam

d. Henry Kissinger

24. What was SALT I?

a. A NATO treaty in response to the Soviet invasion of Afghanistan

b. The first limitation of arms signed between the Soviet Union and the United States

c. A treaty between the United States and China after Sino-Soviet split

d. Charles de Gulle's alternative to NATO after NATO did not help him contain the revolt in French Algeria

25. Which of these is true about economic inequality in the United States since 2000?

a. It has decreased

b. It has stayed the same

c. It was increased

d. It has fluctuated

26. Which of these statements about immigration in the United States is NOT true.

a. Most immigrants into the United States are from Mexico

b. Immigrants often come to the United States to work and earn money

c. Texas has the highest immigrant population

d. It cost more than $20,000 to deport a single person in 2008

27. Which of these is NOT a main reason for the obesity a problem in the United States?

a. Fast food

b. Medications

c. Sedentary lifestyles

d. Social practices

28. Where does the United States get most of its energy from?

a. Coal

b. Nuclear power plants

c. Natural gas

d. Petroleum

29. Which of these is NOT true about No Child Left Behind?

a. It is for disadvantaged students

b. It sets national standards

c. It bases funding off of test scores

d. All of the above

30. Which is NOT true about what the purpose of the Patient Protection and Affordable Care Act (PPACA)?

a. Lower the costs of healthcare for the nation

b. Make health insurance more affordable

c. Make insurance companies offer the same rates to all people regardless of sex or preconditions

d. Everyone being insured

31. Which of these is true about guns in America?

a. Gun violence has been in an incline since the 1990s

b. Most homicides in America are committed with a gun

c. More than half of Americans own at least one gun

d. All of the above are true

32. Which United States president was influential in the peace talks following World War I?

a. Woodrow Wilson

b. William Taft

c. Warren Harding

d. Franklin Roosevelt

33. Which of these was NOT a cause of the Cold War?

    a. Harry Truman's dislike for Joseph Stalin

    b. The United State's fear of Communism

    c. The rivalry between the United States and the Soviet Union during WWII

    d. The Soviet Union's fear of the Atomic Bomb

34. Which of these was NOT a result of World War II?

    a. Germany was split into four parts

    b. The United States emerged as a super power

    c. Britain emerged victorious and economically stable

    d. It increased the power of communist Russia

35. Which of these was NOT an effect of the Cold War?

    a. The United States and Great Britain became the only world superpowers

    b. The collapse of the Soviet Union and communism

    c. The build up of atomic weapons in the United States and the Soviet Union

    d. The Vietnam War

Part II - World History

1. Which leaders were considered "The Big Three" of the Allied countries?

    a. Adolf Hitler, Benito Mussolini and Fumimaro Konoe

    b. Franklin Roosevelt, Winston Churchill and Charles de Gaulle

    c. Joseph Stalin, Franklin Roosevelt and Winston Churchill

    d. Joseph Stalin, Harry Truman and Winston Churchill

2. What was the Non-Aligned Movement?

a. A bloc of nations that did not align itself with the United States or Soviet Union

b. A bloc of nations the United States set up to stand against communism

c. A movement within the United States to become iso-lationist once again

d. A movement within the United states to be more benevolent world-wide instead of taking advantage of third world countries

3. What is MAD?

a. Mutually Assured Defense

b. Military Attack Defense

c. Mutually Assured Destruction

d. Massive Attack Destruction

4. What was the Berlin Blockade?

a. The First Major Crisis of the Cold War

b. The Soviet Union stopped allowing aid to get to Berlin

c. The cause for the Berlin Airlift

d. None of the above

5. What was Détente?

a. A "cooling down" period of the Cold War

b. A "warming up" period of the Col War

c. A period in which the United States was unsure who the leader of Soviet Russia was

d. B and C

6. What was the motive of the Great Game between Russia and Great Britain during the New Imperialism colonization of Asia?

a. To secure clear paths to countries like India, Iran and Afghanistan

b. To financially exhaust the other

c. To establish trade routes across Asia to Japan and Korea

d. To be the first to secure trade agreements with most of Asia

7. What was one thing achieved with the Glorious Revolution in Great Britain in 1688?

a. A Catholic monarch was removed from the throne

b. A new social order demanding economic equality

c. New industrial machines that lowered the cost of goods

d. The standardization of education which allowed everyone to go to school

8. What was the main industry of the Industrial Revolution?

a. Glass

b. Paper

c. Textiles

d. Gas lighting

9. Which was the first European colony to declare its independence?

a. Haiti

b. The United States

c. Chile

d. Mexico

10. Which event is considered to be the start of the French Revolution?

   a. The rise of Napoleon Bonaparte

   b. The Woman's March on Versailles

   c. The passing of The Declaration of the Rights of Man and of the Citizen

   d. The storming of the Bastille

11. Which famous American directly influenced the writing of The Declaration of the Rights of Man and of the Citizen in France?

   a. John Adams

   b. George Washington

   c. Thomas Jefferson

   d. Benjamin Franklin

12. Which of these was NOT a cause of the Bolshevik Revolution?

   a. Lack of technological advancement in agriculture

   b. Lack of education and health care

   c. Spread of Marxist ideas

   d. Inspiration from the American Revolution

13. Which of these was NOT a consequence of the Bolshevik Revolution?

   a. Women in Russia gained the right to vote

   b. Russia became a super power

   c. The Cold War

   d. The royal family went into hiding

14. Which of these was NOT included in the Government of India Act introduced by Britain in 1935?

    a. It set up eleven provincial assemblies that had local control of government

    b. It give India a say in its domestic affairs

    c. It addressed the political disputes between Hindus and Muslims

    d. It introduced direct elections

15. Who is considered to be the founding father of Pakistan?

    a. Muhammad Jinnah

    b. Jawaharial Nehru

    c. Choudhary Rahmat Ali

    d. Mahatma Gandhi

16. Which of these was NOT one of Sun Yat-sen's, president of the Republic of China, Three Principles for the governing of China?

    a. Nationalism

    b. Capitalism

    c. Socialism

    d. Democracy

17. Which of these is NOT true of the Boxer Rebellion in China in 1900?

    a. It failed

    b. It was a peaceful rebellion

    c. It was to expel European powers from China

    d. It was to overthrow the Manchu dynasty

18. What did the Balfour Declaration of 1917 say?

    a. Great Britain had control of Palestine following World War I

    b. Great Britain would support the creation of a Jewish homeland in Palestine

    c. Great Britain would give Palestine to the Arabs at the end of World War I

    d. Arabs and Jews would need to share Palestine

19. What was the Treaty of Sevres of 1920?

    a. A peace treaty that ended the Ottoman Empire after WWI

    b. A treaty by France granting self governance to Syria after WWI

    c. A peace treaty between France and Germany at the end of WWI

    d. A treaty between France and Britain to remain allies following WWI

20. What type of government was instated in Italy under Benito Mussolini in Italy after World War I?

    a. Totalitarianism

    b. Socialism

    c. Democracy

    d. Fascism

21. Who won the Spanish Civil War?

    a. No side one, the war was interrupted by WWII

    b. The Republican Popular Front

    c. The Nationalists led by Francisco Franco

    d. King Alphonso XIII

22. Which of these is NOT true of World War I?

a. It led to the creation of new nations

b. It used modern technology such as guns and tanks

c. It was the result of strong Nationalism in European countries

d. It was fought almost entirely on land

23. What was the immediate cause of WWI?

a. An increased militarism in Europe

b. The murder of Archduke Francis Ferdinand of Austria

c. National rivalries between countries following the Balkan Wars

d. A secret system of alliances between European countries

24. How was the Treaty of Versailles a cause of World War II?

a. It angered many Germans who were willing to look to Hitler to end the Treaty

b. It did not put strict enough ties on Germany's military power

c. It created a system of alliances that dragged multiple countries into WWII

d. It was a peace treaty that prevented any nation from attacking Germany

25. Which of these is NOT a reason that global terrorism has become prevalent?

a. Travel between areas is much easier now

b. Conventional warfare is not viable for less-rich nations

c. Spreading word of ones ideas is easier to do

d. It is easier to be anonymous in the world

26. The Maya are known for their achievements in:

 a. Astronomy and Mathematics

 b. Democratic Government

 c. Agriculture

 d. Sports

27. The alliance linking Russian, France, and Great Britain in 1907 is known as:

 a. The Triple Threat

 b. The Triple Entente

 c. The Entente

 d. The Axis Powers

28. Which countries comprised the Central Powers in World War I?

 a. Germany and Italy

 b. Italy and Austria-Hungary

 c. Austria-Hungary and France

 d. Germany and Austria-Hungary

29. The time period is considered the bridge between the Dark Ages and the Modern era.

 a. The Renaissance

 b. The Medieval Period

 c. The Long Nineteenth Century

 d. The Industrial Revolution

30. What is the rise of new mechanical processes and chemical manufacturing, the development of machine tools, and the rise of steam power is called?

    a. The Mechanical Age

    b. The Iron Age

    c. The Industrial Revolution

    d. The Industrial Iron Age

31. Which country did Germany invade in 1939 that is credited with the start of World War II?

    a. France

    b. Spain

    c. Italy

    d. Poland

32. Which country was not a part of the Axis powers in World War II?

    a. Germany

    b. Italy

    c. Japan

    d. France

33. What were the The Allies of World War II were committed to?

    a. Stopping German aggression

    b., Providing military support to Japan

    c. Providing military equipment to Italy

    d. Trying to capture Hitler alive

34. Which ethnic group could be found in Central Mexico from the 14th to 16th centuries?

a. The Inca

b. The Mayans

c. The Aztec

d. The Olmec

35. Who was the first explorer to circumnavigate the globe?

a. Vasco da Gama

b. Ferdinand Magellan

c. Marco Polo

d. Christopher Columbus

Part II - Geography

1. In which direction has the mainland U.S. expanded since the American Revolution?

a. northward

b. southward

c. eastward

d. westward

2. Which of the following will humans not normally avoid?

a. cold weather

b. warm weather

c. deserts

d. high altitudes

3. Immigrants to the U.S. have always

a. been welcomed with open arms by the native-born population

b. been enslaved

c. been discriminated against before finding equality

d. come from Latin America

4. Diffusion which moves a trend from one leader to another throughout a geographic area is known as

a. expansion diffusion

b. stimulus diffusion

c. relocation diffusion

d. hierarchical diffusion

5. What country has the U.S. military occupied from 2001 until 2011?

a. Afghanistan

b. Iraq

c. Israel

d. Lebanon

6. The science of mapmaking is

a. archaeology

b. cartography

c. geography

d. GPS

7. What is environmental determinism?

a. countries establishing rules to determine land usage

b. human devastation of the environment

c. environments have pre-determined uses which can only be altered by man

d. climate and landforms are responsible for differences in human culture

8. Limited resources generally lead to

a. a dense population

b. exploitation by industrial businesses

c. a trade route

d. a scattered population

9. Which region of the U.S. has the fastest growing population?

a. the northeast

b. the southeast

c. the northwest

d. the Midwest

10. A farmer that produces enough food for his or her family and nothing more is known as a

a. Subsistence farmer.

b. Entrepreneur.

c. Businessman.

d. Migrant farm worker.

11. What is the main reason that food production societies won out over hunting and gathering societies?

a. societies that produce food are more intelligent

b. societies that produce food can support more people

c. societies that produce food have less disease

d. societies that produce food are more mobile

12. Agriculture is best defined as

a. hunting for animals, fishing, or gathering plants

b. deliberate cultivation of plants and raising of animals for food or economic gain

c. the use of technology to increase production

d. altering the genetic material of plants and animals

13. The process by which wild animals were utilized for human benefit is

    a. agriculture.

    b. domestication.

    c. hearth.

    d. agribusiness.

14. Country A has a territory of 5,000 square kilometers with 100 people per square kilometer. Country B has a territory of 10,000 square kilometers with 80 people per square kilometer.

Which country has a higher population?

    a. country A

    b. country B

    c. the populations are equal

    d. there is no way to determine their populations from this information

15. Which of the following countries has the highest population density?

    a. Russia

    b. Canada

    c. India

    d. Turkey

16. Where is Honduras located?

    a. South America

    b. Central America

    c. Asia

    d. Africa

17. What is an epicenter?

a. The spot where an earthquake originates.

b. The spot on the earth's surface directly above where an earthquake originates.

c. The estimated area where an earthquake has taken place.

d. The center of the earthquake.

18. Which lines run east and west around the globe?

a. Longitude

b. Equator

c. Latitude

d. Greenwich Mean Line

19. What is the name of the supercontinent that broke apart to create the continents that we know today?

a. Pangaea

b. Gondwana

c. Ur

d. Laurasia

20. Which country is not a part of the Pacific Rim?

a. United States

b. Japan

c. Australia

d. England

Part III - Social Studies Methods and Concepts

1. What are human constructs that group similar groups of people in one geographic area?

    a. Regions

    b. Countries

    c. Continents

    d. Islands

2. What is the movement of people from rural to urban areas?

    a. Ruralization

    b. Urbanization

    c. Migration

    d. Immigration

3. What are feelings of pride and devotion to your country?

    a. Fanaticism

    b. Jingoism

    c. Nationalism

    d. Absolutism

4. What is one country's domination of another's political and/or economic life?

    a. Capitalism

    b. Socialism

    c. Imperialism

    d. Occupation

5. What are the sum total of an individual's values and attitudes?

    a. Attitude

    b. Identity

    c. Family

    d. Genetic Makeup

6. The ability to understand others because you're able to share their feelings is called:

    a. Sympathy

    b. Pity

    c. Grievance

    d. Empathy

7. Understanding the similarities and differences among various ethnic groups, socioeconomic classes, religions, and other identifying characteristics is called:

    a. Diversity

    b. Range

    c. Empathy

    d. Sympathy

8. Patterns of human behavior (ideas, beliefs, values, etc.) that are transmitted to succeeding generations are called:

    a. Succession

    b. Culture

    c. Evolution

    d. Survival Mechanisms

9. What is the right to select from many alternatives?

    a. Choice

    b. Justice

    c. Alternatives

    d. Live

10. A clash of ideas from incompatible forces is called:

    a. Conflict

    b. Choice

    c. War

    d. Justice

11. Trying to evoke an alteration in ideas or events is trying to elicit _____.

    a. Conflict

    b. Choice

    c. Change

    d. Justice

12. What is the the movement of people to a new country?

    a. Immigration

    b. Migration

    c. Urbanization

    d. Ruralizing

13. What is the movement of people from one place to another, with the purpose of settling either temporarily or permanently called?

    a. Immigration

    b. Migration

    c. Urbanization

    d. Ruralizing

14. What is the process when a minority group slowly adapts to the customs and attitudes of the place or culture that they are in called?

    a. Acculturation

    b. Assimilation

    c. Repatriation

    d. Expatriation

15. What is gaining partial or full control over another country, governing it, while exploiting the country's resources called?

    a. Imperialism

    b. Dictatorship

    c. Colonialism

    d. Revolution

Part IV - Economics

1. The Securities and Exchange Commission regulates

    a. Agriculture

    b. Homeland Security

    c. The national budget

    d. The stock market

2. Federal income tax is

    a. Paid every time you buy something

    b. Paid through fees for government services

    c. Due annually, although it is normally deducted from every paycheck

    d. Due when you receive a government service

3. Which of the following is a good example of a public good?

   a. A park

   b. A plumber

   c. An airline

   d. A taxi

4. Sales tax is

   a. Paid every time you buy something

   b. Paid through fees for government services

   c. Due annually, although it is normally deducted from every paycheck

   d. Due when you receive a government service

5. Which of the following are exempt from federal taxes?

   a. Large corporations

   b. Small businesses

   c. Athletes

   d. Religious institutions

6. The federal government gets its funding by

   a. Taxation

   b. Selling goods

   c. Investing in stocks

   d. Donations

7. During the Great Depression, Keynesian economics was employed to

   a. raise taxes and decrease government spending.

   b. lower taxes and decrease government spending.

   c. raise taxes and increase government spending.

   d. lower taxes and increase government spending.

8. Bank deposits are guaranteed by the

    a. SEC.
    b. FDA.
    c. HUD.
    d. FDIC.

9. If a country's imports have more value than its exports, it is said to have a

    a. trade surplus.
    b. trade deficit.
    c. balance of trade.
    d. globalized economy.

10. What is a tariff?

    a. A tax on imports
    b. A fee for government services
    c. A guaranteed bank deposit
    d. A stock

11. Ideally, supply and demand will settle into

    a. a market.
    b. a mutual fund.
    c.. a balance of trade.
    d. equilibrium.

12. If demand for a product falls sharply when prices rise, the demand has

    a. high elasticity.
    b. low elasticity.
    c. high supply.
    d. low supply.

13. The immediate effect of taxes on a business or a consumer is

    a. an increase in economic efficiency.
    b. a decrease in economic efficiency.
    c. an increase in elasticity.
    d. a decrease in elasticity.

14. When the government increases the money supply and lowers interest rates, it is trying to do what?

    a. slow down the economy

    b. downsize

    c. allow the economy to correct itself naturally

    d. stimulate economic growth

15. If the government raises taxes and decreases spending, it is engaged in what type of policy?

    a. contractionary

    b. expansionary

    c. speculative

    d. stimulus

16. When the price of a good rises, the quantity of a good rises. When the price falls, the quantity falls. What best describes this relationship?

    a. Supply

    b. Demand

    c. Deficit

    d. Inflation

17. What is the ability of an economy to produce more goods and services than during a previous period is called?

    a. Economic Downturn

    b. Economic Growth

    c. Economic Strength

    d. Economic Weakness

18. What is someone who acquires goods and services for use?

    a. User

    b. Seller

    c. Business

    d. Consumer

19. GDP stands for:

    a. Gross Domestic Profit

    b. Great Domestic Profit

    c. Gross Domicile Proceedings

    d. Gross Domestic Pension

20. When a company earns more money than it spends, they have made a _____.

    a. Loss

    b. Expenditure

    c. Profit

    d. Deposit

Answer Key

1. C
The Gilded Age was a satire given by Mark Twain about how the super-rich were a thin gold varnish covering up societies' woes.

Choice A is incorrect; the California Gold Rush happened before the Gilded Age.

Choice B is incorrect; while having gold was a status symbol it was not the reason why the time period was called the Gilded Age.

Choice D is incorrect; gangsters were never known for gilding their enemies.

2. A
A black exodus from the South to the Midwest intensified during the end of reconstruction and the start of Jim Crow laws.

Choice B is incorrect; while European immigrants were immigrating in large numbers during this time period this was not a name given to it.

Choice C is incorrect; Asian immigrants were immigrating during this time period and suffered a lot of discrimination through a general hostility to their culture and through official means by way of the Chinese Exclusion Act and the Gentleman's agreement.

Choice D is incorrect; the creation of reservations ended in the mid-1800s under President Hays, new reservation land would not be added until 1934 under the Indian Reorganization Act.

3. C
With the 19th Amendment Women's Suffrage came into national law in 1919.

Choice A is incorrect; the Seneca Falls Convention was the first women's rights conventions, it did not actually create any laws though.

Choice B is incorrect; the 18th Amendment to the United States Constitution prohibited the manufacture, sale, transport, import, or export of alcoholic beverages.

Choice D is incorrect; Jeannette Rankin was the first women senator in the United States, before all women had the right to vote, but she never had a law named after her.

4. D
Both the French and the United States contributed to building the Panama Canal, though there was about a decade where there was no construction.

Choice A is incorrect; while the French did start construction of the Panama Canal in 1881, they did not complete it.

Choice B is incorrect; the United States finished the Panama Canal in 1914, but they did not start the construction.

Choice C is incorrect; the Spanish did not contribute to building the Panama Canal.

5. C
Secretary of State John Hay proposed the Open Door Policy to his European counterparts to abate any conflict between powers over China in the future.

Choice A is incorrect; no countries willingly lowered tariffs significantly during the early 20th century when the Open Door Policy took effect.

Choice B is incorrect; President Mckinley did not accept ideas from everyone when the Open Door Policy took effect.

Choice D is incorrect; the revolving door is the name coined for people going from government positions to industry positions they were supposed to regulate and vice versa.

6. A
Before the Federal Reserve Act, banks did not have the authority to put money into, or take money out of circulation.

Choice B is incorrect; there has not been a government bank in the United States since 1836, the Second Bank of the United States.

Choice C is incorrect; laws have been fluid over the years on how much cash a bank must have liquid, and will probably continue to be so.

Choice D is incorrect; The United States has taken assets out of private hands and put them in public trusts, but the Federal Reserve Act did not do this.

7. C
The Germans had a submarine blockade of Great Britain and torpedoed many ships, both merchant and passenger liners, angering many Americans and was a major factor in America entering the war.

Choice A is incorrect; the bombing of Pearl harbor is what led the United States into World War II.

Choice B is incorrect; the United States was not allied with either Britain or France.

8. B
To allow the Allies to pay off their debts to the United States, the United States loaned money to Germany so that they could pay off their reparations to the Allies.

Choice A is incorrect; this is the Marshall Plan after World War II.

Choice C is incorrect; the United Sates actually slowed down immigration to the United States instead of increasing it.

Choice D is incorrect; this is the Truman Doctrine after World War II.

9. B
The United States stock market collapse of 1929 caused the downfall of many financial institutions and the start of the Great Depression.

Choice A is incorrect; Prohibition started in the 1920s, the Great Depression did not start until 1929.

Choice C is incorrect; while Germany did default on its loans to the United States after World War I, the Great Depression occurred several years after this event.

Choice D is incorrect; the Dust Bowl happened during the Great Depression, it did not precipitate it.

10. B
World War II reduced unemployment with so many working-class men in the armed forces, and jobs were available for anyone able to take them.

Choice A is incorrect; the Great Depression ended with the start of World War II, but the economy was already recovering, so there is some doubt as to whether it helped end the depression.

Choice C is incorrect; World War II did not exacerbate the Great Depression because the Great Depression ended with the onset of World War II.

Choice D is incorrect; only the ending of the Great Depression is up for debate.

11. D
A culmination of the answers given and a few others were what caused the Great Depression.

Choice A is incorrect; excessive borrowing was partly to blame for causing the Great Depression, but it would not have been as severe if other things had not also happened.

Choice B is incorrect; restricting the amount of money ensured that people would not be able to pay off their debts as easily, but even that by itself would not have caused the Great Depression.

Choice C is incorrect; with people not spending money the economy continued to slump, but that would not have been severe enough to cause the Great Depression.

12. A
The Smoot-Hawley Tariff Act and the many retaliatory tariffs around the world closed down international trade.

Choice B is incorrect; while there were some revolutions in developing nations, they did not have a significant impact on world trade.

Choice C is incorrect; Black Tuesday was the start of the Great Depression.

Choice D is incorrect; fascist groups taking power did not have an effect on world trade.

13. C
Most people who had money in a bank lost it with no compensation during the Great Depression.

Choice A is incorrect; President Roosevelt set up a program to insure banks that is still in existence today.

Choice B is incorrect; President Roosevelt set up a Social Security administration that is still in effect today.

Choice D is incorrect; President Roosevelt repealed prohibition to increase revenue and decrease the amount spent on enforcement.

14. D
The Tennessee Valley Authority still exists as a government utility company, but is not connected with the ending of the Great Depression.

Choice A is incorrect; the Gold Standard was ended during the Great Depression by all first world nations because so many people were demanding gold in exchange for money that governments would go bankrupt otherwise.

Choice B is incorrect; Prohibition was formally ended during the Great Depression due to its unpopularity and the increased revenue and decreased expenditures from enforcement.

Choice C is incorrect; the Dust Bowl ended in 1940 right before the end of the Great Depression.

15. A
Roosevelt started "Fireside Chats" to let the nation know what was happening and relieve their fears.

Choice B is incorrect; while Roosevelt did work with world leaders, but these were not called fireside chats.

Choice C is incorrect; the television was not yet invented.

Choice D is incorrect; while Roosevelt did have many talks with members of industry, these were not his fireside chats.

16. B
The US entered the Pacific War, declaring war on Japan after Japan bombed Pearl Harbor.

Choice A is incorrect; the United States did not enter WWII to support France.

Choice C is incorrect; the United States was not allied with Great Britain.

Choice D is incorrect; that is not why the United States entered WWII.

17. D
The United States dropped atomic bombs on Hiroshima and Nagasaki.

Choice A is incorrect; the United States bombed Hiroshima, but not Osaka.

Choice B is incorrect; the United States bombed Nagasaki, but not Hokkaido.

Choice C is incorrect; the United States did not bomb Osaka or Hokkaido.

18. D
Franklin Roosevelt was president for most of WWII.

Choice A is incorrect; Woodrow Wilson was president during WWI.

Choice B is incorrect; Herbert Hoover was president before WWII.

Choice C is incorrect; Harry Truman was president for the end of WWII.

19. A
The propaganda campaign, Rosie the Riveter, was to encourage women to work in factories producing wartime supplies.

Choice B is incorrect; women did join the military, but Rosie the Riveter did not encourage this.

Choice C is incorrect; Rosie the Riveter did not encourage to support men in the war effort.

Choice D is incorrect; Rosie the Riveter did not encourage woman to product food.

20. B
The allied forces were successful because the United States was able to produce and provide most of the wartime supplies needed to win the war.

Choice A is incorrect; the Allied forces were not more organized.

Choice C is incorrect; the Allied forces did not know all their enemies plans.

Choice D is incorrect; the Allies were not more technologically advanced than the Axis powers.

21. D
Order 9066 forced people of Japanese descent in the United States to be placed in internment camps on the west coast. Choice A is incorrect; African Americans were already allowed to join the military.

Choice B is incorrect; women did serve in the military during WWII, but this Order was unrelated.
Choice C is incorrect; this Order did not relate to Jewish immigration.

22. B
Mikhail Gorbachev, the leader of the Soviet Union, initiated glasnost, or openness, and perestroika, or restructuring, which allowed for the eventual disintegration of the Soviet Union, therefore ending the Cold War.

Choice A is incorrect; while Ronald Reagan does gain a lot of credit for ending the Cold War, his policies hurt the Soviet economy at the cost of hurting the American economy.

Choice C is incorrect; though John Kennedy helped usher in Détente after the Cuban Missile Crisis but died before the ending of the Soviet Union.

Choice D is incorrect; though Khrushchev relaxed many Soviet totalitarian policies he never wanted the Soviet Union to end.

23. B
Choice B is correct, the invasion of Afghanistan led to a boycott of the 1980 Olympics by the United States and a return to deep mistrust between the two countries.

Choice A is incorrect; Nikita Khrushchev helped usher in Détente, but he did not live to see it end.

Choice C is incorrect; the Invasion of Vietnam happened before Détente started and did not end Détente.

Choice D is incorrect; Henry Kissinger helped orchestrate Détente, but did not end it.

24. B
SALT I was a major step for the United States and the Soviet Union toward the limitation, and eventually disarming, of missiles. Though the SALT talks were unsuccessful, they did provide a framework for the future.

Choice A is incorrect; NATO did not sign a treaty in response to the Soviet invasion of Afghanistan, it was just the end of Détente.

Choice C is incorrect; China and the United States did not sign a treaty after the split, but they did come to speaking terms and United States President Richard Nixon visited the country.

Choice D is incorrect; Charles de Galle withdrew France from NATO, but did not make an alternative. France was still part of European Economic Community.

25. C
Incomes of the wealthiest Americans have risen much more than incomes of the poorest Americans.

Choice A is incorrect; it has increased.

Choice B is incorrect; it has increased.

Choice D is incorrect; it increased steadily.

26. C
The only true statement is that California has the highest immigrant population.

Choice A is incorrect; thirty percent of the foreign born population in 2010 came from Mexico.

Choice B is incorrect; the main reason people immigrate to the United States is to escape poverty and earn money.

Choice D is incorrect; the process of deporting someone in 2008 cost more than $23,000.

27. B
Medications are not a leading cause of obesity.

Choice A is incorrect; fast food has a high fat content that can lead to obesity.

Choice C is incorrect; lack of exercise is a leading cause of obesity.

Choice D is incorrect; eating and sedentary activities, such as watching TV, as a way of socializing, increases obesity.

28. A
Coal is America's second leading source of energy, behind oil, and provides for twenty-three percent of U.S. energy consumption. While oil is used primarily for automotive fuel, a vast majority of America's coal is used to produce electricity.

Choice B is incorrect; the United States gets some energy from nuclear power, but not the majority.

Choice C is incorrect; the United States gets some energy from natural gas, but not the majority.

Choice D is incorrect; the United States gets some energy from petroleum, but not the majority.

29. B
There are no national standards for No Child Left Behind, each state develops its own standards.

Choice A is incorrect; disadvantaged students were the main reason No Child Left Behind was implemented.

Choice C is incorrect; funding is based solely on test scores and improvement every year.

Choice D is incorrect; because Choice B is correct.

30. D
Complete coverage for everyone was never a goal believed achievable by PPACA.

Choice A is incorrect; lowering costs was a goal for PPACA

Choice B is incorrect; healthcare in the United States had been unaffordable to many people making them a strain on the system when they did receive healthcare.

Choice C is incorrect; a main problem with health insurance was that the people that needed insurance the most were the ones that least likely could afford.

31. B
Most homicides in America involve guns.
Choice A is incorrect; gun violence has been in decline during that time period.

Choice C is incorrect; a little more than a third of Americans own at least one gun.

Choice D is incorrect; choices A and C are incorrect.

32. A
Woodrow Wilson was president of the United States during WWI and helped establish the League of Nations after WWI.

Choice B is incorrect; William Taft was the president before Wilson.

Choice C is incorrect; Warren Harding was the president after Wilson.

Choice D is incorrect; Franklin Roosevelt was the president during WWII.

33. C
The United States and the Soviet Union were allies during WWII - this was not a cause of the Cold War.

Choice A is incorrect; Harry Truman, the US president, disliked and distrusted Joseph Stalin, the leader of the Soviet Union.

Choice B is incorrect; the US was afraid that the Soviet Union would spread communism to the rest of the world.

Choice D is incorrect; the Soviet Union was afraid of the United State's military power.

34. C
Although victorious, Britain was very economically unstable after WWII.

Choice A is incorrect; Germany was split into four sections controlled by different countries that were part of the Allies.

Choice B is incorrect; the United States made a profit on the war and was a super-power afterwards.

Choice D is incorrect; Russia also became a super-power and began to spread communism.

35. A
Great Britain's economy collapsed after WWII and after the Cold War, the United States was the only world super-power.

Choice B is incorrect; the Soviet Union collapsed after the Cold War because of economic weakness.

Choice C is incorrect; both the Soviet Union and the US created many atomic weapons during the Cold War.

Choice D is incorrect; the US entered the war in Vietnam in an effort to contain communism.

Part II - World History

1. C
Russia, the United States and Great Britain where considered "The Big Three" Allied countries.

Choice A is incorrect; these were the three main leaders of the Axis powers.

Choice B is incorrect; France was not part of "The Big Three" Allied forces.

Choice D is incorrect; Harry Truman was the US president at the end of WWII, but Franklin Roosevelt was the main WWII president.

2. A
The Non-Aligned Movement was a group of nations that wanted to be neutral in the Cold War.

Choice B is incorrect; the United States helped create a few blocs of nations to oppose communism, but none were the Non-Aligned Movement.

Choice C is incorrect; the movement for the United States to become isolationist once again was very small, and not the Non-Aligned Movement.

Choice D is incorrect; there were movements within the United States to become a more worldly benevolent power, but none were called the Non-Alignment Movement.

3. C
Mutually Assured Destruction (MAD) is a doctrine of military strategy and national security policy in which a full-scale use of high-yield weapons of mass destruction by two or more opposing sides would cause the complete annihilation of both the attacker and the defender.

Choice A is incorrect; MAD refers to nuclear weapons, an offensive weapon rather than a defensive one.

Choice B is incorrect; while military in nature that was not the acronym.

Choice D is incorrect; while a good description of what were to happen, this is not the acronym.

4. D
None of the answers are correct.

Choice A is incorrect; while true, it is not the only right answer.

Choice B is incorrect; the Soviet Union stopped aid from getting to Berlin to force the allies to allow them to supply Berlin and thereby gain control of the city, but that is not the only correct answer.

Choice C is incorrect; the Berlin Airlift was able to surpass the quantity of cargo that regularly reached Berlin before the blockade, but it is not the only correct answer.

5. A
Détente is the easing of hostility or strained relations, especially between countries. Here, it refers to was a period during the middle of the Cold War in which both the United

States and the Soviet Union were on cordial terms, and actively trying to lessen tensions.

Choice B is incorrect; there were a couple "warming up" periods in which the world came very close to nuclear war, but these were not Détente.

Choice C is incorrect; the United States usually knew who was the head of the Soviet Union and it never became an issue when they did not.

Choice D is incorrect; neither C nor B are correct.

6. A
By controlling Central and Southern Asia, other countries would be easily accessible.

Choice B is incorrect; neither country was trying to financially exhaust the other.

Choice C is incorrect; neither country was trying to trade with Japan.

Choice D is incorrect; Britain and Russia were not competing for trade in Asia.

7. A
The Catholic King James II of England was overthrown by the Protestant William of Orange.

Choice B is incorrect; the Glorious Revolution did not achieve economic equality.

Choice C is incorrect; implementation of industrial machines was during the Industrial Revolution.
Choice D is incorrect; the Glorious Revolution did not impact education.

8. C
Increased productivity due to the cotton gin, power looms, the flying shuttle and the spinning jenny made textile production the leading industry of the Industrial Revolution

Choice A is incorrect; glass was produced, but it was not the main industry.

Choice B is incorrect; paper was produced, but it was not the main industry.

Choice D is incorrect; gas lighting was produced, but it was not the main industry.

9. B
The United States was the first European colony to declare its independence from Britain in 1776.

Choice A is incorrect; Haiti declared its independence from France in 1804.

Choice C is incorrect; Chile was independent of Spain by 1831.

Choice D is incorrect; Mexico was independent of Spain by 1831.

10. D
The storming of the Bastille happened in July, 1789 and is considered the flash point of the French Revolution.

Choice A is incorrect; Napoleon's rise to power is considered to be the end of the French Revolution.

Choice B is incorrect; the March on Versailles happened during the French Revolution when people were upset with the high price of bread.

Choice C is incorrect; this document was passed in France in August, 1789.

11. C
Thomas Jefferson directly influenced the writing of the Declaration by working with the man who introduced it, General Lafayette.

Choice A is incorrect; John Adams did not directly influence the writing of the Declaration.

Choice B is incorrect; George Washington did not directly influence the writing of the Declaration.

Choice D is incorrect; Benjamin Franklin did not directly influence the writing of the Declaration.

12. D
The American Revolution in 1776 happened much earlier than the Bolshevik Revolution in 1917.

Choice A is incorrect; peasants were upset at having to farm with primitive tools.

Choice B is incorrect; peasants were upset at the lack of social welfare provided by the government.

Choice C is incorrect; the spread of Marxist ideas encouraged people to create new political parties.

13. D
The royal family was placed under house arrest and then killed - they did not go into hiding.

All the other choices were choices were consequences of the revolution, women were given the right to vote, Russia became a world power under Stalin and Lenin and communist ideas spread during the Bolshevik Revolution led to the Cold War with capitalism.

14. C
The Government of India Act introduced by Britain in 1935 did not address how to resolve disputes between Hindus and Muslims.

Choice A is incorrect; the Act did set up provincial governments.

Choice B is incorrect; the Act set up an assembly that gave India a say in most of the country's decisions, but not defense or foreign affairs.

Choice D is incorrect; the Act did set up direct elections.

15. A
Muhammed Jinnah was a Muslim who insisted that a separate state be created for Muslims.
Choice B is incorrect; Jawaharial Nehru was a famous Indian political leader.

Choice C is incorrect; Choudhary Rahmat Ali was a Muslim who helped create Pakistan, but is not considered to be the founding father.

Choice D is incorrect; Mahatma Gandhi was a Indian leader famous for his peaceful protests against the British.

16. B
Yat-sen did not try to promote capitalism in China.

Choice A is incorrect; Sun believed giving China national pride would help free it from foreign rule.

Choice C is incorrect; Sun believed the needs of all people should be met by the people.

Choice D is incorrect; Sun believed China should be democratic.

17. B
The Boxer Rebellion was very violent and many Europeans and Chinese were killed.

Choice A is incorrect; the Boxer Rebellion was eventually crushed by European powers and the Manchus were reinstated in government.

Choice C is incorrect; many Chinese were upset at the amount of control Europe had in China.

Choice D is incorrect; the Manchu government were puppets to the European powers.

18. B
The British Foreign Secretary, Arthur Balfour, promised Palestine to the Jews, in the Balfour Declaration of 1917.

Choice A is incorrect; the League of Nations gave control of Palestine to Britain following World War I.

Choice C is incorrect; Britain promised Palestine to the Arabs in the McMahon Agreement.

Choice D is incorrect; that Arabs and Jews would need to share Palestine was not part of the Declaration.

19. A
The Treaty of Sevres was treaty between the Allies and the Ottoman Empire at the end of WWI that liquidated the Ottoman Empire.

Choice B is incorrect; the Treaty of Sevres was not between France and Syria.
Choice C is incorrect; the Treaty of Sevres was not between France and Germany.

Choice D is incorrect; the Treaty of Sevres was not between France and Britain.

20. D
The dictator Mussolini established a Fascist government in Italy.

Choice A is incorrect; Mussolini did not establish a Totalitarian government in Italy because the Church was still considered to be higher than the government.

Choice B is incorrect; Mussolini did not establish a Socialist government in Italy.

Choice C is incorrect; Mussolini did not establish a Democracy government in Italy.

21. C
The Nationalists won the Spanish Civil War and Franco became a dictator in Spain.

Choice A is incorrect; the Spanish Civil War ended before WWII began.

Choice B is incorrect; the Popular Front lost the Spanish Civil War.

Choice D is incorrect; King Alphonso XIII had previously been exiled to France.

22. D
WWI was fought both on land and at sea.

Choice A is incorrect; new nations were created after WWI such as Austria and Hungary.

Choice B is incorrect; it was one of the first large scale wars to use modern technology which led to larger loss of life and property.

Choice C is incorrect; strong Nationalism in European countries led to hatred of other countries.

23. B
The murder of Archduke Francis Ferdinand of Austria was the spark that set off WWI.

Choice A, C and D are incorrect, these were all causes of WWI, but not the immediate cause.

24. A
The Treaty of Versailles created poverty in Germany, which Hitler sought to change.

Choice B is incorrect; the Treaty of Versailles demilitarized Germany.

Choice C is incorrect; the Treaty of Versailles did not create a system of alliances.

Choice D is incorrect; the Treaty of Versailles did not prevent attacks on Germany.

25. D
It is now much harder to be anonymous in the world due to the advance of technology and social media. One person could be instantly recognizable around the globe from mak-

ing a single video that may or may not be significant. This is not a reason global terrorism has increased.

Choice A is incorrect; in the 21st century it is easier to travel anywhere on Earth than it has ever been.

Choice B is incorrect; with technologically rich nations can destroy less technologically advanced ones without the smaller ones even being able to retaliate.

Choice C is incorrect; spreading ideas is now easier than ever with the advent of the internet.

26. A
The Maya used a numeration system, based on the number 20, which included the concept of zero. The system was based on dots and bars, where one dot represented one and a bar represented five. This bar-dot system, similar to the one used today by computers (1 and 0) is called a binary system. Using these in different positions the Maya were able to make complex calculations, including certain astronomical operations, which they computed with great precision.

The Maya are not know for democratic government, agriculture or sports.

27. C
Russia, France, and Great Britain were known as the Triple Entente during WWI.

Choice A is incorrect. There was no Triple Threat during WWI.
Choice D is incorrect. The Axis Powers existed during WWII.

28. D
Germany and Austria-Hungary were known as the Central Powers.

Choice A and B are incorrect. Italy was an Allied Power.

Choice C is incorrect. France was an Allied Power.

29. A
The Renaissance spanned the time period between the Dark Ages, ending in the 15th century and the beginning of the Early Modern era, starting in the 16th century.

Choice B is incorrect. The Medieval Period was a part of the Dark Ages.

Choice C is incorrect. The Long Nineteenth Century happened after the Early Modern era.

Choice D is incorrect. The Industrial Revolution happened during the nineteenth-century.

30. C
The Industrial Revolution was the period when mechanical processes and manufacturing boomed.

Choice A is incorrect. The Mechanical Age is not a time period that exists.

Choice B is incorrect. The Iron Age began around 1200 BC.

Choice D is incorrect. The Industrial Iron Age does not exist.

31. D
Germany invaded Poland in 1939.

Choice A is incorrect. Germany did not invade France until 1940.

Choice B is incorrect. Spain was generally uninvolved in WWII.
Choice C is incorrect. Italy fought with Germany at the beginning of the war.

32. D
France was an Allied force.

Choice A is incorrect. Germany was an Axis power.
Choices B and C are incorrect. Italy and Japan were Axis
powers.

33. A
The Allies wanted to stop German aggression.

Choice B is incorrect. The Allies opposed Japan.

Choice C is incorrect. The Allies opposed Italy until Italy
became an ally.

Choice D is incorrect. The Allies did not want to capture
Hitler.

34. C
The Aztec existed in Central America from the 14th to the
16th centuries.

Choice A is incorrect. The Inca existed in South America.

Choice B is incorrect. The Mayans existed in Central
America well before the 14th century.

Choice D is incorrect. The Olmec predate the Aztec by
several thousand years.

35. B
Ferdinand Magellan was the first explorer to circumnavigate
the globe.

Choice A is incorrect. Vasco da Gama was the first European
to reach India by sea.
Choice C is incorrect. Marco Polo was a merchant who
traveled to China.

Choice D is incorrect. Christopher Columbus was credited
with first discovering North America.

Part III - Geography

1. D
The U.S. has expanded westward all the way to the Pacific Ocean since the American Revolution.

Choice A is incorrect; Canada is to the north.

Choice B is incorrect; the Caribbean and Mexico were and are to the south.

Choice C is incorrect; the Atlantic Ocean was and is to the east.

2. B
Humans do not normally avoid warm weather.

Choice A is incorrect; humans try to avoid cold weather.

Choice C is incorrect; deserts cannot support very much life.

Choice D is incorrect; high altitudes cannot support much life.

3. C
Immigrants to the U.S. have always been discriminated against before finding equality.

Choice A is incorrect; the native-born population tends not to welcome immigrants.

Choice B is clearly incorrect; slavery has been illegal since 1863.

Choice D is incorrect; immigrants have come from all over the world.

4. D
Diffusion, which moves a trend from one leader to another throughout a geographic area is known as hierarchical diffusion.

Choice A is incorrect; expansion diffusion is the diffusion of people.

Choice B is incorrect but plausible; stimulus diffusion pertains to ideas, but not necessarily to leaders.

Choice C is incorrect; relocation diffusion skips over certain areas.

5. A
The U.S. military occupied Afghanistan since 2001 until June 2011.

Choice B is incorrect; Iraq was invaded in 2003 and U.S. forces have officially left.

Choice C is incorrect; the U.S. has never occupied Israel.

Choice D is incorrect; the US. sent troops to Lebanon in the 1980s, but did not occupy Lebanon.

6. B
The science of mapmaking is called cartography.

Choice A is incorrect; archaeology is the study of human activity in the past.

Choice C is incorrect; geography is a field of science dedicated to the study of the lands, the features, the inhabitants, and the phenomena of the Earth.

Choice D is incorrect; GPS stands for Global Positioning System.

7. D
Environmental determinism is the theory that climate and landforms are responsible for differences in human culture.

Choice A is incorrect; but plausible due to the word "determine."

Choice B is incorrect; human devastation of the environment is an environmental influence on humans.

Choice C is incorrect; this may be true but it is irrelevant to the question.

8. D
Limited resources generally lead to a scattered population, since the area cannot support many people.

Choice A is incorrect; a dense population needs more resources.

Choice B is incorrect; industrial businesses look for an abundance of resources.

Choice C is incorrect; a trade route may appear but this is irrelevant to the question.

9. B
The southeast region of the U.S. has the fastest growing population.

10. A
Subsistence agriculture is self-sufficiency farming in which the farmers focus on growing enough food to feed themselves and their families. The typical subsistence farm has a range of crops and animals needed by the family to feed and clothe themselves during the year.

Choice B is incorrect; entrepreneurs start businesses.

Choice C is incorrect; businesspeople sell things.

Choice D is incorrect; migrant farm workers are employees of other farmers.

11. B
Food production societies won out over hunting and gathering societies because it supports more people.
Choice A is incorrect; food production has no correlation with intelligence.

Choice C is incorrect; societies that produce food actually have had more disease.

Choice D is incorrect; societies that produce food are actually less mobile.

12. B
Agriculture is the science or practice of farming, including cultivation of the soil for the growing of crops and the rearing of animals to provide food, wool, and other products.

Choice A is incorrect; this is the definition of hunting and gathering.

Choice C is incorrect; technology is used, but B is a much better answer.

Choice D is incorrect; plants and animals do get altered in agriculture, but choice B is a much better answer.

13. B
The process by which wild animals were utilized for human benefit is domestication.

Choice A is incorrect; agriculture is too general a term.

Choice D is incorrect; agribusiness began after domestication took place.

14. B
Country A has a territory of 5,000 square kilometers with 100 people per square kilometer.

Country B has a territory of 10,000 square kilometers with 80 people per square kilometer.

Country B would have a population of 800,000 people.

Choice A is incorrect; country A would have population of 500,000 people.

15. C
India has the highest population density.

16. B
Honduras is located in Central America.

17. B
The spot on the surface directly above where the earthquake originates is the epicenter.

Choice A is incorrect. The spot where an earthquake actually originates is located deep underground, and it is not the epicenter.

Choice C is incorrect. The epicenter pinpoints the exact spot on the earth's surface directly above the earthquake, not the general area.

Choice D is incorrect. The epicenter pinpoints the exact spot on the earth's surface directly above the earthquake, not the earthquake's center.

18. C
Latitude lines run east and west around the globe.

Choice A is incorrect. Longitude lines run north and south around the globe.

Choice B is incorrect. The equator is the imaginary line on Earth's surface that divides the Earth into the Northern and Southern Hemispheres.
Choice D is incorrect. The Prime Meridian is 0 degrees longitude.

19. A
Pangaea is the supercontinent that broke apart to create the continents that we know today.

Choice B is incorrect. Gondwana was the name of one of the southern supercontinents that broke off of Pangaea.

Choice C is incorrect. The supercontinent, Ur, predates Pangaea.

Choice D is incorrect. Laurasia was one of the southern supercontinents that broke off of Pangaea.

20. D
England is on the eastern side of the Atlantic Ocean, not a part of the Pacific Rim.

Choice A is incorrect. The western coast of the United States and Hawaii are part of the Pacific Rim.

Choice B is incorrect. Japan is a part of the Pacific Rim.

Choice C is incorrect. Australia is a part of the Pacific Rim.

Part IV - Social Studies Concepts and Methods

1. A
Regions are human constructs that group similar groups of people in one geographic area.

Choice B is incorrect; Countries are artificial borders that group people together. A country is a type of region.

Choice C is incorrect; Continents are very large landmasses.

Choice D is incorrect; Islands are surrounded by water on four sides.

2. B
Urbanization is the movement of people from rural to urban areas.

Choice A is incorrect; Ruralization is the movement of people from urban to rural areas.

Choice C is incorrect; Migration is the temporary or permanent movement by people from one place or another to settle.

Choice D is incorrect; Immigration is the movement of people into a country that they are not native to.

3. C
Feeling pride and devotion to your country is called nationalism.

Choice A is incorrect; Fanaticism involves obsessive enthusiasm for something.

Choice B is incorrect; Jingoism is aggressive foreign policy as a form of extreme patriotism.

Choice D is incorrect; Absolutism is the belief in absolute political, philosophical, and ethical principles.

4. C
One country's domination of another country's political and/or economic life is called imperialism.

Choice A is incorrect; Capitalism is an economic and political system where trade and industry are controlled by private owners.

Choice B is incorrect; Socialism is a social and economic system where the means of production is socially owned.

Choice D is incorrect; Occupation is the activity of living and using a particular place.

5. B
Identity is your own values and attitudes.

Choice A is incorrect; Attitude is the way a person thinks or feels about something.

Choice C is incorrect; Your values do not create your family.

Choice D is incorrect; Your values are not ingrained in your genetic makeup.

6. D
Empathy is your ability to understand others because you're able to share their feelings.

Choice A is incorrect; Sympathy is the act of feeling sorry for someone or something.

Choice B is incorrect; Pity is a strong feeling of sadness for someone or something.

Choice C is incorrect; A grievance is a general feeling of having been treated unfairly.

7. A
Diversity is known as understanding the similarities and differences among various ethnic groups, socioeconomic classes, religions, and other identifying characteristics.

Choice B is incorrect; A range is a group of different things that are similar in some ways.

8. B
Culture is patterns of human behavior (ideas, beliefs, values, etc.) that are transmitted to succeeding generations.

Choice A is incorrect; Succession is a series of things that come one after another.

Choice C is incorrect; Evolution is slow change and/or development.

Choice D is incorrect; Survival mechanisms are behavioral patterns that are selected and reinforced across generations.

9. A
Choice is your right to select from different alternatives.

Choice B is incorrect; Justice happens when individuals are given fair treatment in personal, societal, and governmental interactions.

10. A
Conflict is a clash of ideas from incompatible forces.

Choice B is incorrect; Choice is your right to select from different alternatives.

Choice C is incorrect; War is a prolonged conflict between two parties, usually countries or groups of people.

Choice D is incorrect; Justice happens when individuals are given fair treatment in personal, societal, and governmental interactions.

11. C
Change is trying to evoke an alteration in ideas or events.

Choice A is incorrect; Conflict is a clash of ideas from incompatible forces.

Choice B is incorrect; Choice is your right to select from many alternatives.
Choice D is incorrect; Justice happens when individuals are given fair treatment in personal, societal, and governmental interactions.

12. A
Immigration is the movement of people into a country that they are not native to.

Choice B is incorrect; Migration is the temporary or permanent movement by people from one place or another to settle.

Choice C is incorrect; Urbanization is the movement of people from rural to urban areas.

Choice D is incorrect; Ruralizing is the movement of people from urban to rural areas.

13. B
Migration is the temporary or permanent movement by people from one place or another to settle.

Choice A is incorrect; Immigration is the movement of people into a country that they are not native to.

Choice C is incorrect; Urbanization is the movement of people from rural to urban areas.

Choice D is incorrect; Ruralizing is the movement of people from urban to rural areas.

14. B
Assimilation is defined as when a minority group slowly adapts to the customs and attitudes of the place or culture that they are in.

Choice A is incorrect; Acculturation is the process of cultural change that happens when cultures meet.

Choice C is incorrect; Repatriation is the process of returning a person to the place of citizenship.

Choice D is incorrect; Expatriation is the process of withdrawing from your native country.

15. C
Gaining partial or full control over another country and governing it, while exploiting the country's resources is called colonialism.

Choice A is incorrect; Imperialism is the policy of giving a country power through diplomacy or military force.
Choice B is incorrect; A dictatorship is a country ruled by a dictator.

Choice D is incorrect; Revolution is a change in power that takes place over a short period of time, often by force.

Part V - Economics

1. D
The Securities and Exchange Commission, SEC, regulates The stock market.

Choice A is incorrect; the FDA regulates agriculture.

Choice B is incorrect; the Department of Homeland Security is charged protecting the United States from terrorist attacks.

Choice C is incorrect; congress determines the national budget.

2. C
Federal income tax is due annually, although it is normally deducted from every paycheck.

Choice A is incorrect; sales tax is paid every time you buy something.

Choice B is incorrect; fees are distinct from taxes.

Choice D is incorrect; income tax is distinct from government services.

3. A
A park is a good example of a public good. A public good is a commodity or service that is provided without profit to all members of a society, either by the government or a private individual or organization.

Choices B, C and D are incorrect; a plumber, an airline and a taxi are examples of private services.

4. A
Sales tax is paid every time you buy something.

Choice B is incorrect; fees are distinct from taxes.

Choice C is incorrect; sales tax is paid when you buy something, not annually.

Choice D is incorrect; sales tax is distinct from government services.

5. D
Religious institutions are not subject to federal taxes.

Choices A and B are incorrect; large corporations and small businesses are subject to taxes.

Choice C is incorrect; Athletes are private citizens and are subject to taxes.

6. A
The federal government gets its funding by taxation.
Choice B is incorrect; the government does not sell goods.

Choice C is incorrect; the government rarely invests in stocks.

Choice D is incorrect; the government rarely receives donations.

7. D
During the Great Depression, Keynesian economics prescribed lower taxes and increasing government spending to stimulated the economy.

Choice A is incorrect; this is the opposite of the Keynesian approach.

Choice B is incorrect; government spending was increased during the Great Depression.

Choice C is incorrect; taxes were not raised during the Great Depression.

8. D
Bank deposits are guaranteed by the Federal Deposit Insurance Corporation.

Choice A is incorrect; the SEC regulates the stock market.

Choice B is incorrect; the FDA regulates food and drugs.

Choice C is incorrect; HUD is the department of Housing and Urban Development.

9. B
If a country's imports have more value than its exports, it is said to have a trade deficit.

Choice A is incorrect; a trade surplus is the opposite.

Choice C is incorrect; the balance of trade is the difference between imports and exports.

Choice D is incorrect; globalization simply refers to the connectedness of the world's economies.

10. A
A tariff is a tax on imports.
Choice B is incorrect; a tariff is a tax on imports.

Choice C is incorrect; tariffs have little to do with bank deposits.

Choice D is incorrect; tariffs are not related to stocks.

11. D
Ideally, supply and demand will settle into equilibrium.

Choice A may seem plausible, but market is too general and choice D is a better answer.

Choice B is is irrelevant, but plausible because of the word "mutual."

Choice C is incorrect; balance of trade refers to imports and exports.

12. A
If demand for a product falls sharply when prices rise, the demand has high elasticity. Elasticity is the influence of prices on demand.

Choice B is incorrect; if the demand had low elasticity price would not fall sharply.

Choice C is incorrect; supply is not related.

Choice D is incorrect; supply has little to do with this situation.

13. B
The immediate effect of taxes on a business or a consumer is a decrease in economic efficiency.

Choice A is incorrect; the opposite is true.

Choices C and D are incorrect; elasticity isn't relevant.

14. D
When the government increases the money supply and lowers interest rates, this policy is designed to stimulate economic growth.

Choice A is incorrect; the opposite is true.

Choice B is incorrect; downsizing is unrelated to this situation.

Choice C is incorrect; to allow the economy to correct itself naturally the government would do nothing.

15. A
If the government raises taxes and decreases spending, it is engaged in a contractionary policy.

Choice B is incorrect; expansionary policy lowers taxes and increases spending.

Choice C is incorrect; speculation sounds plausible but has little to do with this situation.

Choice D is incorrect; stimulus would involve expansionary policy.

16. A
Supply is a fundamental laws of economics.

Choice B is incorrect. The law of demand states that when the price of a good rises, its demand falls. When the price falls, the demand rises.

Choice C is incorrect. Having more expenses than income is

a deficit.

Choice D is incorrect. Inflation is the rise in prices relative to the amount of money in circulation.

17. B
The ability of an economy to produce more goods than a previous period is called an economic growth.

Choice A is incorrect. An economic downturn is when the economy starts to slow down.

Choice C is incorrect. Though economic strength is related to the quantity of goods it can produce, does not measure between periods.

Choice D is incorrect. The inability to produce many goods and having a weak economy is considered an economic weakness.

18. D
Consumers acquire goods and services for their use.

Choice A is incorrect. A user uses goods and services, but it is not the correct answer.

Choice B is incorrect. A seller sells goods and services.

Choice C is incorrect. Businesses provide and/or sell goods and services.

19. A
GDP stands for Gross Domestic Profit.

Choice B in incorrect. Great Domestic Profit is not a term that exists.

Choice C is incorrect. Gross Domicile Proceedings is not a term that exists.
Choice D is incorrect. Gross Domestic Pension is not a term that exists.

20. C

When a company earns more than it spends, they make a profit.

Choice A is incorrect. A company makes a loss when they spend more than they earn.

Choice B is incorrect. An expenditure is when a company pays for an expense.

Choice D is incorrect. A deposit is an amount of money put in a bank account.

Conclusion

CONGRATULATIONS! You have made it this far because you have applied yourself diligently to practicing for the exam and no doubt improved your potential score considerably! Getting into a good school is a huge step in a journey that might be challenging at times but will be many times more rewarding and fulfilling. That is why being prepared is so important.

Good Luck!

www.ingramcontent.com/pod-product-compliance
Lightning Source LLC
Chambersburg PA
CBHW072012090426
42740CB00011B/2162